DATE DUE

ECOLOGICAL HOTELS

edited by Patricia Massó

teNeues

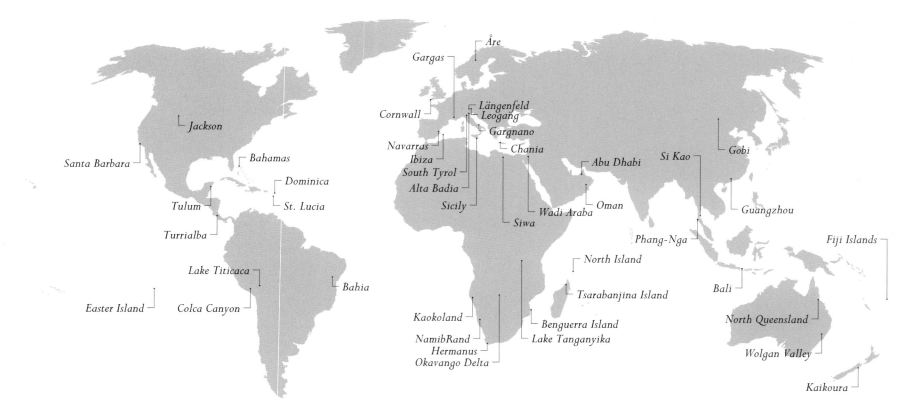

Åre

Gargas

Cornwall

Längenfeld
Leogang

Navarras

Gargnano

Jackson

Chania

Si Kao

Gobi

Santa Barbara

Bahamas

Ibiza
South Tyrol

Abu Dhabi

Dominica

Alta Badia

St. Lucia

Oman

Guangzhou

Tulum

Sicily

Wadi Araba

Turrialba

Siwa

Phang-Nga

Fiji Islands

Lake Titicaca

North Island

Bahia

Bali

Easter Island

Colca Canyon

Tsarabanjina Island

North Queensland

Kaokoland

Benguerra Island

NamibRand

Lake Tanganyika

Wolgan Valley

Hermanus

Okavango Delta

Kaikoura

Ecological Hotels

Introduction

Hotels are becoming green. What began in a small niche that had long gone unnoticed has now become a global trend. More and more hoteliers are discovering their green conscience and building in harmony with nature—using local materials, converting to renewable energy sources, and installing sophisticated water conservation systems—a reaction to a growing demand particularly in lifestyle oriented cities. Values such as environmental compatibility and sustainability also want to be lived when travelling.

The 46 hotels portrayed in this elaborately designed volume are sustainable in many respects: minimizing the harmful effects on the environment, conserving natural resources, being closely linked with their cultural environment, and demonstrating social responsibility.
They whisk us away to tropical island paradises, magical places and sometimes the most remote parts of the world. Hidden in the deepest tropical rainforest, in Costa Rica the Pacuare Lodge (one of the main pioneers of eco-tourism) allows the old dream of mankind of being at one with nature, turn into reality. They set an exemplary model where the world appears in its most fragile state. In the South Seas the Jean-Michel Cousteau Fiji Island Resort is fully involved in the protection of coral reef and the precious underwater world.

Some ultimately let us play Robinson and experience first-hand how our senses are sharpened and our perceptions are altered when television and telephone are not constantly the focus of attention. This helps us to recognise the simple fact—that less can often be more.
In Titilaka in the Andes we are directly confronted with what we lose if we do not take action. Researchers have calculated that Lake Titicaca will silt up with persistent global warming.

In Africa operators of luxury safari camps recognised that eco-tourism means the economic future of the continent. The Beyond Group that has Xaranna Okavango Delta Camp in its portfolio is passionately devoted to the protection of endangered species and has been extremely successful in their resettlement. The Boulders Safari Camp in Namibia allows us to gain a spiritual experience of infinite expanse, with the renaturalization of farmland on a grand scale.

Social projects such as hospitals and schools are often also financed by the room rates. Above all secure jobs are created. On the Caribbean island of Dominica the Jungle Bay Resort benefits an entire region.
Many of the hotels illustrated are becoming places of cultural interaction and allow an authentic view of a foreign culture. In the Australian Daintree Eco Lodge we can learn from the Aborigines to touch the earth gently and to only leave behind a soft footprint.

Now the trend has arrived in the midst of Western societies beyond the tropical paradises, the tree houses in the jungle and the endless nature reserves. Brand new design hotels such as Copperhill Mountain Lodge in North Sweden or the Scarlet on the Cornish coast show that we can protect natural resources and offer sophisticated design at the same time. Perhaps these hotels can become a role model of how we can treat our environment more respectfully in everyday life.

Bärbel Holzberg

Einleitung

Hotels werden grün. Was in einer kleinen, lange wenig wahrgenommenen Nische begann, wurde zum globalen Trend. Immer mehr Hoteliers entdecken ihr grünes Gewissen, bauen im Einklang mit der Natur, nutzen heimische Materialien, rüsten auf erneuerbare Energiequellen um, installieren ausgeklügelte Wassersparsysteme. Sie reagieren damit auf eine steigende Nachfrage gerade bei lifestyle-orientierten Großstädtern. Werte wie Umweltverträglichkeit und Nachhaltigkeit wollen auch beim Reisen gelebt werden.

Die 46 Hotels, die dieser aufwändig gestaltete Bildband vorstellt, sind nachhaltig in vielerlei Hinsicht, indem sie die Belastungen für die Umwelt minimieren, die natürlichen Ressourcen schonen, sich eng mit ihrem kulturellen Umfeld verlinken und soziale Verantwortung übernehmen.
Sie entführen uns auf paradiesische Tropeninseln, an magische Orte und manchmal bis ans Ende der Welt. Verborgen im tiefsten tropischen Regenwald lassen sie den alten Menschheitstraum vom Einssein mit der Natur Wirklichkeit werden, wie die Pacuare Lodge in Costa Rica, einer der großen Pioniere des Ökotourismus. Sie leisten Vorbildliches, wo die Welt am fragilsten scheint. In der Südsee engagiert sich das Jean-Michel Cousteau Fiji Island Resort umfassend beim Schutz der Korallen und der kostbaren Unterwasserwelt.

Manche lassen uns endlich einmal Robinson spielen, uns hautnah erleben, wie sehr unsere Sinne geschärft werden, unsere Wahrnehmung sich verändert, wenn nicht ständig Fernseher und Telefon die Aufmerksamkeit beanspruchen. Sie verhelfen zu der simplen Erkenntnis, dass weniger oftmals mehr sein kann.
Unmittelbar damit konfrontiert, was wir verlieren, wenn wir nicht handeln, wird man im Titilaka in den Anden. Forscher haben errechnet, dass der Titicaca-See bei anhaltender Erderwärmung versanden wird.

In Afrika haben die Betreiber luxuriöser Safari-Camps erkannt, dass der Ökotourismus die ökonomische Zukunft des Kontinents bedeutet. Die Beyond-Gruppe, die das Xaranna Okavango Delta Camp in ihrem Portfolio hat, betreibt intensiven Artenschutz, ist äußerst erfolgreich bei der Wiederansiedlung vom Aussterben bedrohter Tierarten. Das Boulders Safari Camp in Namibia verhilft uns zu dem spirituellen Erlebnis von unendlicher Weite, weil Farmland im ganz großen Stil renaturiert wurde.

Mit den Zimmerpreisen werden oft auch soziale Projekte finanziert, Krankenhäuser und Schulen. Vor allem aber werden sichere Arbeitsplätze geschaffen. Auf der Karibikinsel Dominica profitiert eine ganze Region vom Jungle Bay Resort.
Viele der vorgestellten Hotels werden zu Orten kultureller Interaktion, erlauben den authentischen Blick auf eine fremde Kultur. In der australischen Daintree Eco Lodge kann man von den Aborigines lernen, die Erde nur sanft zu berühren, einen nur sachten Fußabdruck zu hinterlassen.

Nun ist der Trend jenseits der Tropenparadiese, der Baumhäuser im Dschungel, der unendlichen Naturreservate mitten in den westlichen Gesellschaften angekommen. Brandneue Designhotels wie die Copperhill Mountain Lodge im Norden Schwedens oder das Scarlet an der Küste Cornwalls zeigen, dass man die natürlichen Ressourcen schonen und trotzdem anspruchsvoll gestaltet sein kann. Vielleicht können genau diese Hotels zum Vorbild dafür werden, wie wir zurück im Alltag einen sorgsameren Umgang mit unserer Umwelt pflegen können.

Bärbel Holzberg

Introduction

Les hôtels se mettent au vert. Ce qui avait commencé comme une activité marginale d'une petite niche de marché, longtemps ignorée d'ailleurs, est devenue entre-temps une tendance mondiale. Toujours davantage d'hôteliers découvrent leur sensibilité « verte » et construisent dans le respect de l'environnement en utilisant des matériaux autochtones, en choisissant une alimentation énergétique renouvelable et en installant des systèmes performants pour économiser l'eau. Ils répondent ainsi à une demande toujours croissante de la part des urbains des grandes villes, en quête d'une modification de leur mode de vie. L'on veut voyager dans le respect de ses valeurs comme la non-pollution et le respect de la durabilité.

Les 46 hôtels présentés dans cet ouvrage magnifiquement illustré pratique la durabilité sous de nombreux aspects, en réduisant la pollution de l'environnement, en préservant les ressources naturelles, en se fondant étroitement avec leur environnement culturel et en assumant ses responsabilités sociales.
Ils nous entraînent vers des îles tropicales paradisiaques, vers des coins insoupçonnés et même, quelquefois, jusqu'au bout du monde ! Cachés au plus profond de la forêt tropicale, ils permettent à l'homme de réaliser son rêve atavique d'union avec la nature, comme le Pacuare Lodge en Costa Rica, l'un des plus importants pionniers en tourisme écologique. Ils servent d'exemple là où le monde semble le plus fragile. L'Island Ressort Jean-Michel Cousteau s'est engagé dans les mers du Sud à assurer la protection complète du corail et du merveilleux monde sous-marin.

Quelques-uns nous permettent même de nous croire Robinson Crusoé, de nous faire sentir combien nos sens se voient aiguisés et notre perception de la réalité modifiée, dès lors que la télévision et le téléphone ne requièrent pas continuellement notre attention. Ils permettent de constater que quelquefois peu peut être synonyme de beaucoup! Titilaka, dans les Andes, nous confrontera directement avec la perception réelle de ce que nous perdons si nous n'agissons pas immédiatement. Des chercheurs ont calculé que le lac de Titicaca s'asséchera en cas d'augmentation du réchauffement climatique.

En Afrique, les exploitants du campement de safari de haut de gamme ont reconnu que le tourisme écologique représente l'avenir écologique du continent. Le groupe Beyond, exploitant du Xaranna Okavango Delta Camp, pratique la protection intensive des espèces et récolte de nombreux succès dans la réintroduction d'espèces animales menacées d'extinction. Le Boulders Safari Camp en Namibie nous permet de vivre l'expérience spirituelle de l'immensité, car les terres cultivées ont bénéficié d'une remise en l'état naturel de grande envergure.

Le tarif des chambres sert très souvent à financer des projets sociaux, des hôpitaux ou des écoles. Mais il permet surtout d'assurer des emplois. Dans les Caraïbes, toute une région de l'île de Saint-Domingue profite du Jungle Bay Resort.
Nombre de ces hôtels présentés opèrent localement une interaction culturelle et permettent de jeter un regard différent et authentique sur une autre culture. Les aborigènes australiens nous enseignent, dans le Daintree Eco Lodge, comment ne pas interférer dans la nature et ne laisser qu'une légère empreinte de notre passage.

La tendance dans la société de consommation occidentale est à présent aux paradis tropicaux, aux fermes dans la jungle, aux réserves naturelles aux extensions illimitées. De tous nouveaux hôtels design, comme le Copperhill Mountain Lodge dans le Nord de la Suède ou le Scarlet sur la côte de Cornwall, sont la preuve que l'on peut protéger les ressources naturelles tout en réalisant des aménagements de haute qualité. Peut-être ces hôtels pourront-ils nous servir de modèle pour nous enseigner comment préserver notre environnement dans notre vie quotidienne.

Bärbel Holzberg

Introducción

Los hotelen se están haciendo „verdes". Lo que empezó como un pequeño nicho de mercado al que durante tiempo se le prestó poca atención, se ha convertido en una tendencia generalizada. Cada vez más hoteleros descubren su conciencia ecológica, construyen en armonía con la naturaleza, aprovechan materiales locales, se adaptan a las fuentes de energía renovables e instalan sistemas inteligentes de ahorro de agua. Ésta es la reacción a la creciente demanda del estilo de vida de los habitantes de las grandes ciudades, que también cuando viajan quieren vivir valores como la sostenibilidad y el respeto del medio ambiente.

Los 46 hoteles que han sido seleccionados para este cuidado volumen son sostenibles en muchos sentidos, ya que minimizan el impacto medioambiental, cuidan los recursos naturales, se relacionan estrechamente con su entorno cultural y asumen responsabilidades sociales.
Nos transportan a paradisiacas islas tropicales, a lugares mágicos y a veces hasta el fin del mundo. El viejo sueño de la humanidad de fusionarse con la naturaleza se hace realidad, oculto en lo más profundo de la selva tropical, como en el Pacuare Lodge de Costa Rica, uno de los grandes pioneros del turismo ecológico. Allí donde el Mundo es más frágil, estos hoteles constituyen un ejemplo. En los Mares del Sur, el resort Jean-Michel Cousteau en las islas Fiji se dedica de lleno a la protección de los corales y los valiosísimos fondos marinos.

Por fin se nos permite jugar por una vez a ser robinsones, experimentar cómo se nos agudizan los sentidos y cambia nuestra percepción de la realidad, cuando no tenemos que prestar constante atención al teléfono y a la televisión, ayudándonos a entender que con frecuencia menos puede ser más.
En Titilaka, en Los Andes, nos confrontamos de inmediato con lo que podemos perder si no ponemos remedio. Los investigadores han calculado que el Lago Titicaca se va a colmatar por el continuo calentamiento global.

En África, los propietarios de lujosos campamentos para safaris se han dado cuenta que el turismo ecológico constituye el futuro económico del continente. El Grupo Beyond, propietario del Hotel Xaranna Okavango Delta Camp, realiza una intensiva labor de protección de la biodiversidad y una exitosa reintroducción de especies animales en peligro de extinción. En el Boulders Safari Camp de Namibia podemos gozar la esperiencia espiritual de la gran inmensidad, pues la granja se ha renaturalizado de una manera soberbia.

Con el importe de las habitaciones se financian con frecuencia proyectos sociales, hospitales y escuelas. Sobre todo, se crean puestos de trabajo seguros. En la caribeña Isla Dominica, el resort Jungle Bay beneficia a toda la región.
En muchos de estos hoteles se produce una interacción cultural y permiten una auténtica visión de una cultura diferente. En Daintree Eco Lodge se puede aprender de los aborígenes a tocar la tierra con suavidad y a dejar una ligera huella tras de sí.

La tendencia de construir casas en los árboles de la selva ha llegado ahora a la sociedad occidental, lejos de los paraísos tropicales. Hoteles de diseño de nueva creación como el Copperhill Mountain Lodge en el norte de Suecia o el Scarlet, en la costa de Cornualles, muestran que se pueden cuidar los recursos naturales y a la vez disfrutar de una refinada decoración. Quizá estos hoteles nos puedan servir de ejemplo de cómo cuidar mejor el medio ambiente de vuelta a la vida cotidiana.

Bärbel Holzberg

Introduzione

Gli hotel diventano ecologici. Tutto è cominciato con piccole iniziative per molto tempo considerate di nicchia, ma oggi si può parlare di tendenza globale. Sono sempre più numerosi gli albergatori che riscoprono la loro sensibilità ecologica, costruiscono edifici nel pieno rispetto della natura, adoperano materiali del luogo, utilizzano per le forniture fonti di energia rinnovabili, installano sistemi perfezionati per risparmiare acqua. Si tratta di soddisfare in questo modo una domanda sempre più crescente da parte di persone che abitano in grandi centri urbani e che desiderano riorganizzare il loro stile di vita. Il rispetto per l'ambiente e l'uso di materiali a lunga durata sono valori che non si devono trascurare nemmeno quando si è in viaggio.

I 46 hotel presentati in questo prezioso volume fotografico sono progettati proprio per poter durare a lungo, poiché riducono notevolmente l'impatto sul territorio, risparmiano le risorse naturali, creano stretti legami con il loro ambiente culturale e si assumono anche delle responsabilità sociali.
Ci si allontana e si evade su isole che sono autentici paradisi tropicali, in luoghi magici e talvolta fino al punto più estremo della terra. Nascosti nel cuore della foresta tropicale realizzano l'antico sogno dell'uomo di sentirsi tutt'uno con la natura; così per esempio accade nel Pacuare Lodge in Costa Rica, una delle prime grandi strutture nel settore dell'eco-turismo. Questi hotel vengono gestiti in maniera esemplare proprio là dove la terra e l'ambiente sono più fragili e delicati. Il Jean- Michel Cousteau Fiji Island Resort, nel Mare del Sud, si sta impegnando in modo notevole per la salvaguardia dei coralli e del prezioso mondo sottomarino.

Alcuni di essi ci fanno sentire novelli Robinson almeno per una volta e ci fanno sperimentare sulla nostra pelle come possano essere affinati i nostri sensi e come cambia la nostra percezione quando non ci sono televisori e telefoni che assorbono continuamente la nostra attenzione. Semplicemente ci aiutano a riconoscere che spesso il poco può essere tanto.
Il lago Titicaca nelle Ande ci propone proprio il problema di cosa perdiamo se non facciamo nulla per l'ambiente. Alcuni ricercatori hanno calcolato che la sua superficie si prosciugherà gradualmente a causa del crescente aumento del riscaldamento della terra.

In Africa i proprietari di campi-safari di lusso hanno riconosciuto che l'eco-turismo può rappresentare il futuro economico del continente. Il gruppo Beyond, che ha nel suo portfolio lo Xaranna Okavango Delta Camp, si impegna con determinazione nella protezione delle specie ed è riuscito infine a realizzare con successo un programma di reinsediamento di specie animali in via di estinzione. Il Boulders Safari Camp in Namibia ci consente di vivere un'esperienza quasi spirituale negli spazi sconfinati grazie ad un grandioso programma di rinaturalizzazione delle terre coltivate.

Con i prezzi delle camere spesso si finanziano anche progetti sociali, ospedali e scuole. Ma soprattutto si creano posti di lavoro sicuri. Sull'isola caraibica di Dominica un'intera regione ha potuto ricevere benessere economico dal Jungle Bay Resort.
Molti degli hotel qui presentati sono diventati luogo per un'interazione culturale e consentono uno scambio autentico con una cultura straniera. Nel Daintree Eco Lodge in Australia si può imparare dagli aborigeni a creare un contatto con la terra che sia lieve e delicato e, nella natura, a lasciare un'impronta impercettibile.

Dai paradisi tropicali, dalle case sugli alberi nella giungla, dalle sconfinate riserve naturali questa tendenza oggi è arrivata anche nel cuore della società occidentale. Nuovissimi hotel di design come il Copperhill Mountain Lodge nel nord della Svezia o lo Scarlet sulla costa della Cornovaglia sono la dimostrazione che si possono sfruttare le risorse naturali senza per questo rinunciare a progettare ambienti raffinati. Forse proprio questi hotel potrebbero essere di esempio per capire come anche nella nostra vita quotidiana potremmo comportarci in modo più responsabile verso l'ambiente.

Bärbel Holzberg

Copperhill Mountain Lodge

Åre, Sweden

No less a figure than a star architect, Peter Bohlin, designer of Apple stores, designed Copperhill Mountain Lodge, which opened at the end of 2008 in the far north of Sweden. Situated at the peak of the 730 meter high Mount Förberget, you'll enjoy a fantastic panoramic view of the mountains and the lakes of Jämtland. The 112 room resort in the largest skiing region in Scandinavia can certify its extensive involvement in environmental management – energy saving programmes, the use of recyclable materials, and the geothermal energy for heating without CO_2 emissions.

Kein Geringerer als Stararchitekt Peter Bohlin, Designer der Apple Stores, entwarf die Ende 2008 eröffnete Copperhill Mountain Lodge im hohen Norden Schwedens. Auf dem Gipfel des 730 Meter hohen Förberget gelegen, eröffnet sich ein fantastischer Panoramablick auf die Berge und Seen Jämtlands. Das 112-Zimmer-Resort im größten Skigebiet Skandinaviens lässt sich sein umfassendes Engagement im Umweltmanagement – Energiesparprogramme, Verwendung recycelbarer Materialien, Heizen mittels Erdwärme ohne CO_2-Emission - zertifizieren.

Le designer des Apple Stores, un célèbre architecte et pas des moindres, Peter Bohlin, a conçu le Copperhill Mountain Lodge, inauguré fin 2008 dans le grand nord de la Suède. Une magnifique vue panoramique vous attend au sommet du mont Förberget (730 m) d'où vous pourrez admirer les montagnes et les lacs du comté de Jämtland. Le centre de vacances de 112 chambres, installé dans le plus grand domaine skiable de la Scandinavie, a demandé la certification de son engagement tous azimuts pour sa gestion de l'environnement, son programme d'économie d'énergie, l'utilisation de matériaux recyclables et de son système de chauffage à géothermie sans émission de CO_2.

Nada menos que el famoso arquitecto Peter Bohlin, diseñador de la tienda Apple, ideó a finales del 2008 el Hotel Copperhill Mountain Lodge en la parte alta del norte de Suecia. Situada en la cima del Förberget, a 730 metros , muestra una fantástica vista panorámica de los montes y el lago Jämtlands. El fuerte compromiso medioambiental del Hotel, que tiene 112 habitaciones y está situado en la zona de esquí de Escandinavia, está certificado en sus programas de ahorro de energía, utilización de materiales reciclables y calefacción mediante energía geotérmica sin emisión de CO_2.

E' il famoso designer Peter Bohlin, noto per aver disegnato i magazzini della Apple, che ha progettato il Copperhill Mountain Lodge, aperto alla fine del 2008 nel profondo nord della Svezia. Situato sulla cima del Förberge, alto 730 metri, il lodge spazia su una fantastica veduta panoramica sulle montagne ed i laghi dello Jämtlands, nel più vasto comprensorio sciistico della Scandinavia. Con le sue 112 camere, questo resort ha certificato il suo impegno totale nella gestione del rispetto dell'ambiente – programmi di risparmio energetico, uso di materiali riciclabili, riscaldamento alimentato da energia geotermica, senza emissioni di CO_2.

The interior design is inspired by the history of the region that traditionally lived off copper mining.

Das Interior Design ist von der Historie der Region inspiriert, die früher vom Kupferbergbau lebte.

La décoration et l'aménagement intérieur sont entièrement inspirés de l'histoire des mines de cuivre implantées dans la région.

El diseño interior está inspirado en la historia de la región, que antiguamente vivía de las minas de cobre.

Il design degli interni si ispira alla storia della regione che prima viveva della produzione mineraria di rame.

16　Copperhill Mountain Lodge　*Åre, Sweden*

The Scarlet

Cornwall, United Kingdom

Opened in September 2009, The Scarlet is enthroned on a cliff top above the dramatically beautiful Cornish coast. The three sisters who own the hotel are behind the sophisticated ecological concept. The hotel spaces and water are heated by a biomass boiler and solar panels. The rainwater tops up the natural pool and toilets are flushed using a grey water harvesting system. They even have a sustainability director. All of these very effective measures and eco-conscious measures contribute to the stylish and modern look of the hotel.

Auf einer Klippe über der dramatisch-schönen Küste Cornwalls thront das im September 2009 eröffnete Scarlet. Drei Schwestern als Besitzerinnen stehen hinter dem ausgefeilten ökologischen Konzept. Die Elektrizität wird von Windkraft erzeugt, geheizt wird mit Biomasse und Solarenergie, Regenwasser füllt Pools und die Toilettenspülung wird mit wiederaufbereitetem Abwasser betätigt. Man leistet sich sogar eine Nachhaltigkeitsdirektorin. Und all diese in der Masse sehr wirkungsvollen Maßnahmen hindern das brandneue Hotel nicht daran, stylisch und modern zu wirken.

Sur un rocher situé au-dessus de la baie de Cornwalls, d'une beauté époustouflante, trône depuis septembre 2009 l'hôtel The Scarlet. Les propriétaires, trois sœurs, sont à la base du concept écologique particulièrement étudié. L'électricité est produite par l'énergie éolienne, le chauffage est assuré par la biomasse et énergie solaire, l'eau de pluie remplit les piscines et les citernes des toilettes profitent de l'eau résiduelle nettoyée. La direction a même engagé une responsable de la durabilité. Et toutes ces mesures très efficaces dans l'ensemble, n'empêchent pas ce tout nouvel établissement d'avoir une apparence moderne et de bon goût!

El Hotel Scarlet, abierto en septiembre de 2009, se encuentra sobre un acantilado en la impresionante y preciosa costa de Cornualles. Las tres hermanas propietarias siguen un refinado concepto ecológico. La electricidad se genera con energía eólica, la calefacción con biomasa y energía solar, el agua de lluvia llena las piscinas y las cisternas de los servicios se llenan con agua reprocesada. Incluso se permiten tener una directora de sostenibilidad. Y todas estas eficaces medidas no impiden que el hotel parezca elegante y moderno.

Lo Scarlet, aperto nel settembre del 2009, si erge sulla scenografica scogliera della Cornovaglia. L'idea di creare una perfetta struttura ecologica è stata delle tre sorelle proprietarie dell'hotel. L'elettricità è prodotta da un impianto eolico, il riscaldamento sfrutta l'energia delle biomasse e panelli solari, le piscine si riforniscono di acqua piovana e le toilette di acqua riciclata. In questo modo, tutti i servizi sono organizzati per poter durare a lungo nel tempo e, al contempo, danno al nuovissimo hotel uno stile architettonico moderno.

From the sweeping terraces with their modern loungers you get a terrific view of the spectacular surfing beaches in Cornwall.

Von den weitläufigen Terrassen mit ihren modernen Liegen bietet sich ein grandioser Blick auf die spektakulären Surferstrände Cornwalls.

Depuis les grandes terrasses équipées de chaises longues au design moderne, le client a une formidable vue panoramique sur les plages de surf les plus spectaculaires de Cornwall.

Desde las terrazas dobles con sus modernas tumbonas, se puede disfrutar de una vista extraordinaria de las espectaculares playas para surf de Cornualles.

Dalle ampie terrazze dall'arredo moderno si apre una grandiosa vista sulle spettacolari spiagge della Cornovaglia, meta degli amanti del surf.

Naturhotel Waldklause

Längenfeld, Austria

The scent of larch wood, spruce wood, fir and Swiss pine wood fill the hotel. These four native wood species were used to build the first wooden hotel in Tirol in a contemporary fashion with ecological aspects in mind. The beds in the 50 rooms have been placed in a lowered area in front of the room which has a wide panoramic window. As you lay in bed the snow-covered tree tops of the near 3,000 metre high Five Finger Peak appear within reach while down below you hear the sounds of the fish creek.

Überall im Haus duftet es behaglich nach Lärchen-, Fichten,- Tannen- und Zirbenholz. Nach den vier heimischen Holzarten, aus denen das erste Holzhotel Tirols nach baubiologischen Gesichtspunkten in einem zeitgemäßen Design errichtet wurde. Die Betten in den 50 Zimmern wurden in einen abgesenkten Bereich vor die zimmerbreite Fensterfront platziert. Im Bett liegend scheinen die schneebedeckten Baumwipfel der knapp 3000 Meter hohen Fünffingerspitze zum Greifen nah, drunten hört man den Fischbach rauschen.

Une odeur de mélèze, de sapin, d'épicéa et de pin embaume l'établissement. L'odeur est caractéristique des quatre types de bois autochtones dans lesquelles ce premier hôtel en bois du Tyrol a été construit, avec tout le confort moderne, mais dans le respect des conséquences biologiques de la construction. Les lits de ses 50 chambres ont été placés dans un espace situé en contrebas, juste devant les larges baies vitrées. Couché dans le lit, la cime enneigée du Fünffingerspitze, culminant à 3 000 m d'altitude, semble être à portée de la main. En contrebas, les eaux d'un ruisseau poissonneux rugissent.

En todo el lugar se respira un agradable aroma a madera de pino, alerce, pícea y abeto; a los cuatro tipos de madera local con la que se construyó el primer Hotel de madera del Tirol de diseño moderno y construcción biológica. Las camas de las 50 habitaciones están situadas frente a las ventanas, de modo que desde la cama se pueden contemplar las cimas nevadas situadas a casi 3000 metros de altitud como si estuvieran al alcance de la mano, mientras se escucha el agua del arroyo con peces de abajo.

Il profumo accogliente del legno di larice, di abete rosso, di abete e di cembro pervade tutti gli ambienti dell'hotel. Con questi quattro tipi di legname, tipici della zona, è stato costruito questo che è il primo hotel del Tirolo realizzato in legno, secondo i criteri della bioarchitettura e con un design attuale. I letti delle 50 camere sono stati collocati in un abbassamento del pavimento, davanti alla vetrata della finestra che occupa l'intera larghezza della parete. Osservandole dal letto le cime innevate dei boschi sul Fünffingerspitze, alto quasi 3000 metri, sembrano così vicine da poterle toccare. Dal basso, invece, si riesce a sentire il mormorio del ruscello.

Modern upholstered furniture in bright colours set a cheerful tone. Large glass windows allow light to flood the chimney hall and corridors.

Moderne Polstermöbel in kräftigen Farben setzen fröhliche Akzente. Große Glasfenster lassen Licht durch Kaminhalle und Gänge fluten.

Des meubles rembourrés modernes, aux couleurs vives, donne un ton joyeux à l'ensemble. De grandes baies vitrées permettent à la lumière de pénétrer dans la salle de la cheminée et dans les couloirs.

Modernos muebles tapizados en colores fuertes aportan un alegre acento. Las grandes cristaleras dejan pasar la luz a través de los pasillos y espacios con chimenea.

I mobili imbottiti moderni e in colori forti danno una nota di vivacità. Le grandi vetrate delle finestre lasciano fluire la luce dal salone con il camino ai corridoi.

Priesteregg

Leogang, Austria

Life on the alpine pasture without the hardships that mountain life can entail—this is promised by Priesteregg (opened in December 2009). The 16 alpine chalets were built 1100 metres high on a mountain plateau in the Salzburg region, offering a panoramic view over the Leoganger Steinbergen range and the Steinerne Meer Mountains. The fact that cars are banned from the idyllic alpine village underlines the nostalgic charm. The chalets have been built from Swiss pine and natural stone. Old forgotten fruit varieties such as Pinzgauer apples and pears are grown in the gardens.

Leben auf der Alm, aber ohne die Mühsal, die das Bergleben mit sich bringen kann, verspricht das im Dezember 2009 eröffnete Priesteregg. Die 16 Almhütten wurden in 1100 Meter Höhe auf ein Hochplateau im Salzburger Land gebaut und bieten einen weiten Blick über die Leoganger Steinberge und das Steinerne Meer. Dass Autos aus dem idyllischen Almdorf verbannt sind, unterstreicht den nostalgischen Charme. Die Gästechalets wurden aus Zirbenholz und Naturstein erbaut, in den Bauerngärten werden alte, vergessene Obstsorten kultiviert, wie die Pastorenbirne oder der Paradiesapfel.

Vivre dans les prairies alpestres, mais sans les difficultés inhérentes à la vie en montagne. Voici ce que promet le Priesteregg, inauguré en décembre 2009. Les 16 chalets d'alpages ont été construits à 1100m d'altitude, sur un haut plateau du Pays de Salzbourg. Ils offrent une large vue sur le Leoganger Steinberge et le Steinerne Meer. Les voitures sont interdites de séjour dans ce village de montagne idyllique et cela ne fait qu'en souligner le charme nostalgique. Les chalets ont été construits en bois de pin et en pierre naturelle. D'anciennes variétés de fruits sont cultivées dans les vergers environnants, telle que la poire des pasteurs ou la pomme du paradis.

El Hotel Priesteregg, constuido en diciembre de 2009, ofrece la vida en los pastos alpinos sin las incomodidades de la vida en la montaña. Las 16 cabañas están construidas a 1100 metros de altitud, en una meseta alta de la región de Salzburgo y ofrecen una amplia vista de las montañas Leoganger Steinberge y Steinerne Meer. El que los coches estén desterrados de este idílico pueblo, subraya el encanto nostálgico. Los alojamientos son de madera de pino y piedra y en las huertas se cultivan olvidados tipos de frutas como las peras de pastor y las manzanas del paraíso.

Vivere in alta montagna ma senza la fatica che può comportare la vita di montagna: ecco cosa condsente questo hotel, aperto nel mese di dicembre 2009. Le 16 baite sono state costruite a 1100 metri di altitudine, su un altopiano nella regione del Salzburg ed offrono un'ampia veduta sulle montagne del Leoganger e sullo Steinerne Meer. Il fascino nostalgico ed idilliaco è accentuato dal fatto che le auto sono completamente bandite dal piccolo paesino di montagna. Gli chalets per gli ospiti sono stati costruiti con legno di cembro e pietra viva, negli orti si coltivano antiche qualità di frutta ormai dimenticate, come le pere vescovo o le mele paradiso.

Blazing open fires make the atmosphere in the comfortable cabins even cosier.

Lodernde Kaminfeuer machen das Ambiente in den komfortablen Hütten noch behaglicher.

Une flambée dans la cheminée rend l'ambiance encore plus chaleureuse dans ces chalets confortables.

Ardientes fuegos de chimenéa hacen que el ambiente de las cómodas cabañas resulte todavía más agradable.

Nelle baite dotate di ogni confort il fuoco scoppiettante nel camino rende l'ambiente ancora più accogliente.

Rock walls integrated in the village houses have become a distinguished design element.

In die Dorfhäuser integrierte Felswände wurden zum charaktervollen Gestaltungselement.

Les parois en pierre des maisonnettes du village contribuent à donner un cachet tout particulier à l'ensemble.

En las casas del pueblo se integran paredes de roca como elemento decorativo que imprime carácter.

L'elemento che più caratterizza questo luogo sono le pareti di pietra viva inserite nella struttura delle abitazioni.

Verdura Golf & Spa Resort

Contrada Verdura Sciacca, Sicily, Italy

Embedded in a hilly landscape descending gently to the sea with lemon and olive groves on Sicily's Southwest coast is where the first resort in the Rocco Forte Collection was built. Set in 230 hectares of grounds the resort offers its guests space and expanse which is a rare find in densely populated Europe. The architecture is consistently modern and clear and the flat roofs of the guest bungalows have been turned green. Coast protection programmes prevent erosions, solar panels provide electricity, and only electric cars are allowed on the resort itself.

Eingebettet in eine sanft zum Meer abfallende Hügellandschaft mit Zitronen- und Olivenhainen an der Südwestküste Siziliens wurde das erste Resort der Rocco Forte Collection gebaut. Mit einem 230 Hektar großen Gelände bietet es seinen Gästen Raum und Weite, wie man es im dicht besiedelten Europa nur selten findet. Die Architektur ist konsequent modern und klar, die flachen Dächer der Gästebungalows wurden begrünt. Küstenschutzprogramme verhindern Erosionen, Sonnenkollektoren liefern den Strom, das Resort selbst darf nur mit Elektroautos befahren werden.

Sur la côte sud-ouest de la Sicile, niché au cœur d'un paysage vallonné couvert de citronniers et d'oliviers, sur une légère pente s'inclinant vers la mer, émerge le premier complexe hôtelier de la Rocco Forte Collection. Sur un terrain de 230ha, il propose à ses clients l'espace suffisant pour qu'ils oublient la densité de population habituelle en Europe. L'architecture est moderne et lumineuse, les toits plats des bungalows ont été peints en vert. Les programmes de protection des côtes empêchent les érosions, les panneaux solaires fournissent l'électricité et seuls des véhicules électriques peuvent circuler sur le site.

El primer resort del Rocco Forte Collection está construido en un paisaje de colinas que caen ligeramente hacia el mar, con limoneros y olivares, en la costa sudoeste de Sicilia. Con un terreno de 230 hectáreas, ofrece a sus huéspedes un espacio tan amplio que ya es difícil de encontrar en la concurrida Europa. Por ello, la arquitectura es moderna y clara y los tejados planos de los bungalows de los clientes están cubiertos de vegetación. Los programas de protección costera evitan la erosión, las placas solares proporcionan la energía y en el hotel sólo se pueden conducir coches eléctricos.

Situato in un paesaggio collinare di uliveti e limonaie che digradano dolcemente verso il mare, sulla costa sud-occidentale della Sicilia, questo è il primo resort della Rocco Forte Collection. La sua area si estende per 230 ettari ed offre ad i suoi ospiti un'ampiezza di spazi come soltanto raramente si trovano in Europa, dove ormai il territorio è densamente abitato. L'architettura è moderna e semplice, i tetti piatti dei bungalows per gli ospiti sono stati ricoperti di verde. Progetti elaborati per contrastare il fenomeno dell'erosione proteggono la costa, collettori di energia solare forniscono la corrente elettrica necessaria, nel resort si possono adoperare soltanto auto elettriche.

Olga Polizzi, *the sister of Sir Rocco Forte, conceived of the design that carries the theme of generous space across all areas of the resort.*

Olga Polizzi, *die Schwester Sir Rocco Fortes, entwarf das Design, das in allen Bereichen die Großzügigkeit des Resorts thematisiert.*

Le design *conçu par Olga Polizzi, la sœur de Sir Rocco Fortes, témoigne dans tous les domaines de l'amplitude du complexe.*

Olga Polizzi, *la hermana del Señor Rocco Fortes, lo diseñó haciendo incapié en la generosidad del espacio en todos los ámbitos.*

Olga Polizzi, *la sorella di Sir Rocco Forte ha curato il design che rende grandiosi tutti gli spazi.*

42   Verdura Golf & Spa Resort *Contrada Verdura Sciacca, Sicily, Italy*

Lefay Gargnano

Gargnano, Italy

The Limonaias—lemon groves that give the landscape on the western shores of Lake Garda its own unique character—provided the model for the architecture of the luxury hotel Lefay, opened in 2008. Minimization of harmful effects on the environment was ensured early on in construction, as power is generated from renewable energy sources and the materials are left as near to their natural state as possible. Luxury is defined by the owner's family as an interaction of space, rest, time, and nature: Everything that contributes to your wellbeing, instead of that which appears fancy.

Die Limonaias, Zitronengärten, die der Landschaft am Westufer des Gardasees ihren ganz eigenen Charakter verleihen, lieferten das Vorbild für die Architektur des 2008 eröffneten Luxushotels Lefay. Auf die Minimierung schädlicher Umwelteinflüsse wurde schon in der Bauphase geachtet, Strom kommt aus erneuerbaren Energiequellen, verwendete Materialien wurden möglichst naturbelassen. Luxus wird von der Besitzerfamilie definiert als ein Zusammenwirken von Raum, Ruhe, Zeit und Natur: Alles, was das Wohlbefinden steigert, nicht einfach nur das, was vordergründig glitzert.

Les Limonaias, ces plantations de citronniers, impriment ce caractère tout particulier au paysage du rivage ouest du lac de Garde. Ils sont à l'origine de l'architecture de l'hôtel de luxe Lefay ouvert en 2008. Déjà dans la phase de construction, l'on a pris soin de minimiser les influences externes négatives, l'électricité est fournie par des sources énergétiques renouvelables et les matériaux naturels utilisés n'ont pas subi, dans la mesure du possible, de transformation. La famille, propriétaire de l'établissement, définit le luxe comme la conjonction d'espace, de calme, du temps et la nature: tout ce qui contribue au bien-être, pas simplement ce qui miroite au premier abord.

Limonaias, jardines de limoneros que caracterizan el paisaje de la costa oeste del Lago de Garda, fueron la fuente de inspiración para la arquitectura del lujoso hotel Lefay, abierto en 2008. Ya en la fase de construcción se intentó minimizar al máximo el impacto medioambiental: la electricidad proviene de fuentes de energía renovables y dentro de lo posible se ha intentado utilizar materiales naturales. La familia propietaria define el lujo como una combinación de espacio, tranquilidad y naturaleza; todo lo que realmente proporciona bienestar y no sólo lo que brilla superficialmente.

Le limonaie, giardini di alberi di limoni che caratterizzano in modo singolare il paesaggio sulla sponda occidentale del Lago di Garda, sono il modello che ha ispirato l'architettura di questo hotel di lusso, aperto nel 2008. Già dalla fase di costruzione è stato elaborato e rispettato un progetto che riducesse al minimo l'impatto nocivo sull'ambiente, la corrente elettrica viene prodotta da fonti di energia rinnovabili e, per quanto possibile, sono stati adoperati materiali allo stato naturale. La famiglia dei proprietari usa definire il lusso come il prodotto dell'incontro tra spazio, tranquillità, tempo e natura: tra tutto ciò che accresce il benessere, dunque, e non semplicemente tra ciò che luccica esteriormente.

The infinity pool offers a dream view, from the 11 hectare hotel park covered with olive groves, to Lake Garda.

Vom Infinitypool eröffnet sich ein Traumblick über den 11 Hektar großen mit Olivenbäumen bestandenen Hotelpark bis zum Gardasee.

Depuis l'immense piscine de l'hôtel, vous apprécierez une fabuleuse vue sur l'oliveraie de 11ha du parc de l'hôtel et s'étendant jusqu'au lac de Garde.

Desde la piscina Infinity podemos disfrutar de una vista de ensueño sobre el parque del hotel, de 11 hectáreas de olivos, hasta el Lago de Garda.

Dalla piscina Infinity si spazia su una veduta da sogno sul parco dell'hotel con i suoi 11 ettari di uliveto e fino al lago di Garda.

Lagació Mountain Residence

San Cassiano, Alta Badia, South Tyrol, Italy

The respect for nature alone ensures people's survival in the Ladin Gader Valley. The Mountain Residence, opened in December 2009, seeks to embody this attitude towards life. In the 24 apartments contemporary design is successfully combined with elements of Alpine tradition. Fragrant Swiss pine, spruce and larch wood provide comfort. Large panoramic windows bring the Dolomite peaks into the rooms. Heat insulation and a compact design aligned to the sun give the hotel the certified climate house A-status.

Allein der Respekt vor der Natur sicherte den Menschen im ladinischen Gadertal das Überleben. Ausdruck dieses über Jahrhunderte gewachsenen Lebensgefühls will die im Dezember 2009 eröffnete Mountain Residence sein. In den 24 Apartments geht zeitgemäßes Design mit alpenländischen Traditionselementen eine geglückte Verbindung ein. Duftendes Zirben-, Fichten- und Lärchenholz sorgt für Behaglichkeit. Großflächige Panoramafenster holen die Dolomitengipfel in die Zimmer. Wärmedämmung und eine kompakte, nach der Sonne ausgerichtete Bauweise verschaffen dem Hotel den zertifizierten Klimahaus A-Status.

Seul le respect pour la nature a permis aux hommes de survivre dans le Val Badia, de langue ladine. La preuve de cette forme de vie, expérimentée au cours des siècles, se veut être la Mountain Residence, inaugurée en décembre 2009. Les 24 appartements, aménagés dans un design contemporain et combiné à des éléments traditionnels alpestres, offrent un heureux contraste. Des arômes de bois de pin des montagnes, d'épicéa et de mélèze donnent un sentiment de bien-être. De grandes baies vitrées panoramiques permettent aux cimes des Dolomites de s'inviter dans les chambres. Le calorifugeage et un mode de construction compacte, orientée vers le soleil, ont permis à cet établissement de recevoir le certificat d'établissement climatique dans la catégorie « A ».

Sólo el respeto de la naturaleza aseguraba la supervivencia humana en el ladino Val Gardena. Mountain Residence, abierto en diciembre de 2009, desea ser el reflejo de este concepto vital que se ha desarrollado a lo largo de los siglos. En los 24 apartamentos hay una atractiva combinación de diseño moderno y elementos tradicionales de Los Alpes. El olor de la madera de pino, de la pícea y alerce es muy placentero. Desde las enormes ventanas panorámicas de las habitaciones se pueden contemplar las cumbres de Las Dolomitas. El hotel cuenta con un certificado de clase A como casa bioclimática por su aislamiento térmico y su robusto estilo de construcción que aprovecha el sol.

L'unica risorsa che ha permesso la sopravvivenza dell'uomo nella regione ladina della Val Gardena è stata il rispetto della natura. Il Mountain Residence, aperto nel dicembre del 2009 vuole appunto essere espressione di questa sensibilità che si è sviluppata nei secoli. Nei 24 appartamenti il design contemporaneo riesce a trovare la giusta combinazione con gli elementi della tradizione alpina. Il profumo del legno di cimbro e di larice rende gli ambienti accoglienti. Le grandi finestre panoramiche delle camere sembrano avvicinare le cime delle Dolomiti. Un sistema utilizzato per trattenere il calore e la posizione dell'edificio, orientato verso il sole, hanno consentito al residence di ricevere il certificato di edificio climatico di livello A.

Fossil findings in display cases with the room numbers refer to the million year old geological heritage of the Alps.

Fossilien-Fundstücke in Vitrinen mit den Zimmernummern verweisen auf das Millionen Jahre alte geologische Erbe der Alpen.

Des objets archéologiques fossilisés, exposés dans les vitrines avec les numéros de chambre, témoignent de l'héritage géologique des Alpes et remontant à des millions d'années.

Los fósiles de las vitrinas con los números de habitación atestiguan la milenaria herencia geológica de Los Alpes.

Pezzi di fossile ritrovati durante i lavori ed esposti in vetrina con il numero della camera corrispondente sono la testimonianza della millenaria struttura geologica delle Alpi.

Hotel Aire de Bardenas

Navarras, Spain

The Southeastern part of Navarra on the edge of the national park of Bardenas Reales is like a barren moonscape. As a result, the hotel designed by Barcelona architects Emiliano Lopez and Monica Rivera resembles a moon settlement. Eight Cubist white buildings are grouped around a main building. The strong winds that gave the hotel its name are held off by recycled wood containers. The deep alcoves—referred by the architects as habitable windows—allow the boundaries to flow (inside and outside).

Einer kargen Mondlandschaft gleicht der südöstliche Teil von Navarra am Rande des Nationalparks Bardenas Reales. Konsequent, dass das Hotel der Barcelonaer Architekten Emiliano Lopez und Monica Rivera einer Mondsiedlung gleicht. Acht kubistische weiße Bauten gruppieren sich um ein Hauptgebäude. Die starken Winde, die dem Hotel seinen Namen gaben, werden von recycelten Holzcontainern abgehalten. Bewohnbare Fenster, wie die Architekten die tiefen Nischen nennen, lassen die Grenzen von Innen und Außen fließend werden.

Cette partie de la Navarre, située au sud-ouest, sur les bords du parc naturel de Bardenas Reales, ressemble à un paysage lunaire aride. Il était donc logique de penser que cet hôtel, conçu par les architectes barcelonais Emiliano López et Monica Rivera, ressemble à une colonie lunaire. Huit constructions cubiques blanches se regroupent autour d'un bâtiment central. Les forts vents, à l'origine du nom de l'hôtel, sont arrêtés par des conteneurs de bois recyclés. Les fenêtres habitables, c'est ainsi que dénomment les architectes ces profondes niches, sont les frontières coulissantes séparant l'intérieur de l'extérieur.

La zona sudoeste de Navarra, junto al parque nacional de las Bardenas Reales, se asemeja a un árido paisaje lunar. Por ello, el hotel de los arquitectos barceloneses Emiliano Lopez y Monica Rivera parece una urbanización lunar. Ocho construcciones cúbicas blancas se agrupan al rededor del edificio principal. Los fuertes vientos a los que el hotel debe su nombre, se retiene mediante unos contenedores de madera reciclado. Ventanas habitables, como llaman los arquitectos a los profundos nichos, hacen que se difuminen las fronteras entre interior y exterior.

Il paesaggio nella parte a sud-est di Navarra, all'estremità del parco nazionale di Bardenas Reale, somiglia ad un arido paesaggio lunare. Allo stesso modo anche l'hotel degli architetti barcellonesi Emiliano Lopez e Monica Rivera somiglia ad una base lunare. Otto edifici bianchi a forma di cubo sono raggruppati intorno ad una struttura principale. Cassoni frangivento in legno riciclato trattengono le forti correnti d'aria che danno il nome all'hotel. Le finestre abitabili, così vengono chiamate dai loro architetti le enormi nicchie, contribuiscono a sfumare la linea di confine tra interno ed esterno.

Minimalism as a theme gives the 22 room hotel its Zen-like character.

Reduktion als Leitmotiv verleiht dem 22-Zimmer-Hotel einen Zen-artigen Charakter.

Le minimalisme est le maître mot qui confère son caractère zen unique à ces 22 chambres d'hôtel.

La reducción como eje central, le proporciona a este hotel de 22 habitaciones un carácter Zen.

Il leitmotiv della riduzione all'essenzialità caratterizza lo stile zen delle 22 camere dell'hotel.

Quilibria Aguas de Ibiza

Santa Eulalia, Ibiza, Spain

In the party district of Ibiza a five-star hotel demonstrates that coolness and sustainability does not necessarily present a contradiction. The hotel, open since 2008, manages to use 35 percent less energy than comparable hotels in the luxury segment through efficiency and the use of renewable energy sources. A Domotics control system allows highly efficient light and temperature settings in the 112 rooms. The sprawling private terraces of the nine penthouse apartments overlook the marina of Santa Eulalia.

In der Partyhochburg Ibiza ist ein Fünf-Sterne-Hotel angetreten zu zeigen, dass Coolness und Nachhaltigkeit kein Widerspruch sein muss. Das 2008 eröffnete Hotel schafft es, durch Effizienz und Nutzung erneuerbarer Energien 35 Prozent weniger Energie zu verbrauchen als vergleichbare Hotels im Luxussegment. In den 112 Zimmern erlauben Domotics, ein Steuerungssystem, besonders sparsame Licht- und Temperatureinstellungen. Von den ausladenden Privatterrassen der neun Lofts in der obersten Etage schaut man über die Marina von Santa Eulalia.

Ibiza, ce haut lieu de la fête et des réjouissances, propose un hôtel de cinq étoiles qui démontre que le calme et la durabilité ne sont pas des notions antagoniques. Cet établissement, ouvert en 2008, a réussi à consommer 35% d'énergie en moins que d'autres hôtels comparables de son segment, grâce à l'efficacité et à l'utilisation d'énergies renouvelables. La domotique installée dans les 112 chambres permet un réglage particulièrement économe de la lumière et de la température. Les généreuses terrasses privées des neuf lofts installés dans les étages supérieurs, offrent une vue spectaculaire sur la marina de Santa Eulalia.

En Ibiza, meca de la fiesta, hay un hotel de cinco estrellas que muestra que los conceptos de modernidad y de sostenibilidad no tienen por qué ser contradictorios. El hotel, que abrió en 2008, logra gastar un 35% menos de energía que hoteles de lujo comparables, mediante la eficiencia y el aprovechamiento de energías renovables. En las 112 habitaciones, la domótica permite seleccionar una temperatura e iluminación especialmente ahorrativas. Desde las despejadas terrazas privadas de los nueve Lofts del piso superior se puede contemplar la Marina de Santa Eulalia.

Sull'isola di Ibiza, regina della mondanità, non si può non segnalare questo hotel a cinque stelle, dimostrazione evidente che la vanità e la capacità di durare a lungo non sempre sono in contraddizione. Grazie ad un programma di efficienza e di impiego di energie rinnovabili, l'hotel, aperto nel 2008, riesce a consumare il 35 % di energia in meno rispetto ad altri hotels dello stesso segmento. Le 112 camere sono dotate della moderna tecnologia della domotica, un sistema di dispositivi di controllo che consente di regolare la temperatura e l'illuminazione in modo da risparmiare energia. Dalle ampie terrazze private dei 9 lofts all'ultimo piano si scorge la Marina di Sant'Eulalia.

All rooms are designed using the principles of Feng Shui. Calm colors and spiral lamps contribute to a feeling of wellbeing.

Sämtliche Zimmer sind nach Feng Shui-Prinzipien gestaltet. Ihre ruhige Farbgebung, wie auch die Lampen in Spiralform sollen zum Wohlbefinden beitragen.

Toutes les chambres sont aménagées selon les règles du Feng Shui. Les coloris atténués ainsi que les lampes en forme de spirale doivent contribuer au bien-être.

Todas las habitaciones están concebidas siguiendo los principios de Feng Shui. Sus relajantes colores y las lámparas con forma helicoidal contribuyen a aumentar el bienestar.

Tutte le stanze sono arredate secondo i principi del feng shui. I colori tranquilli alle pareti e le lampade a forma di spirale contribuiscono ad un senso di benessere.

Adrère Amellal

Siwa, Egypt

An eight hour journey along a dusty road west of Cairo in the oasis of Siwa brings you to perhaps the most unusual hotel in Egypt—a location ideal for leaving the outside world behind. Built from Kershaf, a mix of salt stone, clay, and straw, the lodge blends in with its environment. The buildings (with the 40 rooms furnished in Berber style) are situated together on the salt mountain to which the lodge owes its name: Adrere Amellal means white mountain in the Berber language. Rooms are illuminated by candle light at night because there is no electricity.

Acht staubige lange Fahrstunden westlich von Kairo in der Oase von Siwa liegt das vielleicht ungewöhnlichste Hotel Ägyptens. Ein Ort, wie geschaffen, die Außenwelt ganz weit hinter sich zu lassen. Gebaut aus Kershaf, einer Mischung aus geriebenem Salzstein, Lehm und Stroh, geht die Lodge eine organische Verbindung mit ihrer Umgebung ein. Die Gebäude mit den 40 im Berberstil eingerichteten Zimmern drängen sich an den Salzberg, welcher der Lodge den Namen gab: Weißer Berg – nichts anderes heißt Adrere Amellal in der Berbersprache. Nächtens erhellen Kerzen die Räume, denn es gibt keinerlei Elektrizität.

Cet hôtel, certainement le plus inhabituel d'Égypte, est situé dans l'oasis de Siwa, à l'ouest du Caire, après huit heures de route poussiéreuse. Ce lieu semble être conçu pour laisser le monde extérieur bien loin derrière vous. Construit en kershaf, matériau composé de minerai de sel râpé, argile et paille, l'établissement entre en communion organique avec son environnement. Les bâtiments, abritant 40 chambres aménagées dans le style berbère, sont construits sur les flancs de la montagne de sel à l'origine du nom de la résidence : Montagne blanche, voilà la signification de Adrere Amallal, dans la langue berbère. Des chandelles illuminent les espaces la nuit venue, car l'électricité y est inconnue.

A ocho kilómetros en coche por caminos polvorientos al oeste de El Cairo, en el Oasis de Siwa, se encuentra el quizás más inusual hotel de Egipto. Un lugar que parece creado para dejar atrás el mundo exterior. Construido con la técnica de Kershaf, una mezcla de barro, paja y roca de sal molida, el pabellón establece una unión orgánica con su entorno. El edificio, con 40 habitaciones decoradas con estilo beréber, está a los pies de una montaña de sal, que da nombre al lugar: Montaña Blanca, significado de Adrere Amellal en beréber. Las velas iluminan las estancias, pues no hay ningún tipo de electricidad.

Ad ovest del Cairo, dopo otto ore di viaggio su una pista di sabbia, si giunge all'oasi di Siwa e qui si trova quello che forse è il più insolito hotel dell'Egitto. Un luogo dove si riesce a dimenticare completamente il mondo esterno. Costruito in kershaf, una miscela di salgemma in polvere, argilla e paglia, il lodge riesce a inserirsi in modo del tutto organico nell'ambiente circostante. Gli edifici, con le loro 40 camere arredate in stile berbero, si concentrano ai piedi della montagna di sale che ha dato il suo nome al lodge: „montagna bianca", infatti significa „adrere amellal" in lingua berbera. Di notte gli ambienti sono illuminati dalle luci delle candele perchè qui non c'è elettricità.

The design of the interior rooms reflect the impressive barrenness of the surrounding desert landscape.

Die Gestaltung der Innenräume nimmt die eindrucksvolle Kargheit der umgebenen Wüstenlandschaft auf.

L'aménagement intérieur des espaces est d'une parcimonie impressionnante et correspond au paysage désertique environnant.

La decoración de los espacios interiores transmite la impresionante aridez del paisaje desértico circundante.

L'allestimento degli spazi interni richiama, con la sua semplicità, il fascino del deserto circostante, con il suo paesaggio disadorno.

Feynan Ecolodge

Dana Biosphere Reserve, Wadi Araba, Jordan

Jordan's Dana Biosphere Reserve covers three hundred and twenty square kilometres. Endangered species such as the Syrian wolf or the finely marked desert cats are protected from extinction here. The RSCN (Royal Society for the Conservation of Nature) built the 26 room Ecolodge to generate revenue to protect nature, while at the same time providing employment opportunities to the local Bedouin community. It has become the model for further eco-tourism projects in Jordan.

Dreihundertzwanzig Quadratkilometer umfasst Jordaniens Biosphärenreservat Dana. Vom Aussterben bedrohte Tierarten werden hier geschützt, wie der Syrische Wolf oder die fein gezeichnete Wüstenkatze. Um Stiftungsgelder zu akquirieren und mehr noch, den hier ansässigen Beduinen einen sicheren Arbeitsplatz zu bieten, hat die verantwortliche RSCN (Royal Society for the Conservation of Nature) die 26 Zimmer umfassende Eco Lodge gebaut. Sie ist zum Prototyp für weitere Öko-Tourismus Projekte in Jordanien geworden.

Dana, la réserve de biosphère de la Jordanie, possède une extension de 320 km². Les espèces animales menacées d'extinction y sont protégées, tel le loup syrien ou le chat des sables aux fines rayures. Pour recevoir des dons et, bien plus encore, pour assurer aux Bédouins autochtones un poste de travail, la RSCN (Royal Society for the Conservation of Nature) a construit cette résidence hôtelière écologique de 26 chambres. Elle doit devenir le prototype d'autres projets de tourisme écologique en Jordanie.

Dana, reserva de la biosfera de Jordania, abarca trescientos kilómetros cuadrados. Aquí se protegen animales en vías de extinción, como el lobo sirio o el delicadamente llamado gato del desierto. La RSCN (Real Sociedad para la Conservación de la Naturaleza) ha construido este alojamiento ecológico, que consta de 26 habitaciones, para recibir dinero de las fundaciones y, entre otras cosas, ofrecer un puesto de trabajo estable a los beduinos asentados en la zona. Es el prototipo para futuros proyectos de turismo ecológico en Jordania.

La riserva naturale della biosfera di Dana, in Giordania, si estende per 320 chilometri quadrati. Qui sono protette specie animali in via di estinzione come il lupo siriano o il grazioso gatto del deserto. Per raccogliere fondi e acquisire donatori e ancor più per offrire un posto di lavoro sicuro ai beduini che si sono insediati nella zona, la società responsabile della gestione RSCN (Royal Society for the Conservation of Nature) ha costruito questo Eco Lodge, con 26 camere. Si tratta di un progetto prototipo che aprirà la strada ad altri progetti di eco-turismo in Giordania.

Simplicity is the style principle of the lodge and the focus is on the protection of nature.

Einfachheit ist Stilprinzip der Lodge. Der Schutz der Natur, die man mit dem Mountainbike erkunden kann, steht im Vordergrund.

La simplicité est le principe stylistique de ce complexe hôtelier. La protection de la nature est placée en premier lieu. La découverte des environs se fait en VTT.

El principio del estilo del alojamiento es la sencillez. Aquí reina la protección de la naturaleza, que se puede descubrir en bicicleta de montaña.

La semplicità è alla base dello stile del lodge. Massima importanza qui viene data alla tutela della natura che si può esplorare in mountain bike.

70   Feynan Ecolodge *Dana Biosphere Reserve, Wadi Araba, Jordan*

Qasr Al Sarab Desert Resort

Liwa Desert, Abu Dhabi, United Arab Emirates

The Liwa desert is the largest sand desert in the world. The red golden dunes tower up to 200 meters high. The Anantara Group opened its second hotel in Abu Dhabi in this endless expanse. The old fortifications of the desert country are used as a model for the architecture. An Experience Center educates guests about the sensitive ecosphere of the desert landscape. The rare Oryx Gazelle can be sighted on excursions in the Emirates' largest nature reserve, which spans 3000 square kilometres.

Die Liwa-Wüste ist die größte zusammenhängende Sandfläche in unserer Welt. Bis zu 200 Meter türmen sich die rot-goldenen Dünen auf. In dieser unendlichen Weite hat die Anantara-Gruppe ihr zweites Haus in Abu Dhabi eröffnet. Als Vorbild für die Architektur dienten die alten Festungsbauten des Wüstenstaats. Ein Experience Center will Gäste mit der sensiblen Ökosphäre der Wüstenlandschaft vertraut machen. Bei Exkursionen in das mit 3000 Quadratkilometer größte Naturreservat der Emirate kann man die seltene Oryx Gazelle beobachten.

Le désert de Liwa est la plus grande étendue de sable d'un seul tenant au monde. Les dunes, teintées d'ocre et d'or, atteignent près de 200m de hauteur. Dans cette étendue infinie, le groupe Anantara a inauguré son deuxième établissement à Abou-Dhabi. Les vieilles fortifications de ce pays du désert ont servi de modèles pour son architecture. Un centre d'expérimentation veut faire connaître aux clients la délicate écologie des paysages du désert. Des excursions dans la plus grande réserve naturelle de l'émirat, avec une extension de près de 3000 km², permettent d'observer une espèce rare : l'oryx gazelle.

El desierto de Liwa es la mayor extensión de arena del mundo. Las dunas doradorojizas se elevan hasta los 200 metros. En esta extensión sin límite, el Grupo Anantara ha abierto su segunda casa en Abu Dhabi. La fuente de inspiración de esta arquitectura son las antiguas fortalezas de la ciudad del desierto. El objetivo del centro de experiencias es familiarizar al visitante con la sensible esfera ecológica del paisaje desértico. En las excursiones en la mayor reserva natural de los Emiratos, con 3000 kilómetros cuadrados, se puede obsevar la rarísima gacela Orix.

Il deserto Liwa è la più estesa superficie sabbiosa del mondo. Le dune di sabbia rosso-dorata possono ergersi fino a 200 metri. In questo luogo sconfinato il gruppo Anantara ha aperto il suo secondo hotel ad Abu Dhabi. L'architettura ha preso a modello le antiche fortificazioni del paese. Un Experience Center consentirà agli ospiti di entrare in contatto e di familiarizzare con la delicata ecosfera del paesaggio desertico. Durante le escursioni in questa che con i suoi 3000 chilometri quadrati è la più grande riserva naturale degli Emirati Arabi, si può anche osservare la rarissima gazzella oryx.

Opulent fabrics and artistically handmade furniture with 1800 original paintings impart a piece of authentic Arabian heritage to the 206 rooms and suites.

Opulente Stoffe, kunstvoll handgefertigte Möbel und 1800 Originalgemälde vermitteln in den 206 Zimmer und Suiten ein Stück authentisches arabisches Erbe.

De riches étoffes, de beaux meubles artisanaux et 1800 tableaux originaux transmettent dans les 206 chambres et suites une part de l'authentique héritage arabe.

Tejidos opulentos, artísticos muebles hechos a mano y 1800 pinturas originales, transmiten una parte de la auténtica herencia árabe en las 206 habitaciones y suites.

Materiali sfarzosi, pregiati mobili rifiniti a mano e 1800 quadri originali tramandano agli ospiti delle 206 camere e suites un pezzo di autentica eredità araba.

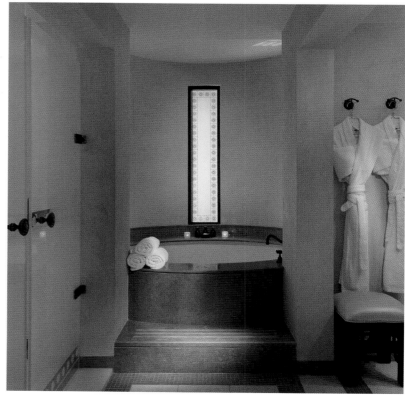

Six Senses Hideaway Zighy Bay

Musandam Peninsula, Oman

On the one side are the rugged rocks of the Hadschar mountains with their deep valleys, while on the other, the 1.6 kilometre long sandy beach of Zighy Bay. The location for the first Six Senses Hideaway in the Middle East could not be better. The 82 villas have been built in traditional Oman style. The interior design is inspired by Arabian culture, yet without any excessive splendor. The detailed Environment Management Program monitors the respectful treatment of the environment.

Auf der einen Seite die zerklüfteten Felsen des Hadschar-Gebirges mit ihren tief eingeschnittenen Tälern, auf der anderen Seite der 1,6 Kilometer lange Sandstrand der Zighy Bay am nördlichen Zipfel der Halbinsel Musandam: Die Lage für das erste Six Senses Hideaway im Mittleren Osten könnte nicht besser sein. Die 82 Villen wurden im traditionellen Oman-Stil gebaut. Das Interior Design ist inspiriert von der arabischen Kultur, verzichtet allerdings auf jeden aufdringlichen Prunk. Das detaillierte „Environment Management Program" wacht über den schonenden Umgang mit der Umwelt.

Les rochers déchiquetés des montagnes de l'Hadschar avec leurs vallées fortement encaissées, d'un côté, et 1,6km d'une longue plage de sable de la baie de Zighi à la pointe nord de la presqu'île de Musandam, de l'autre côté : la situation du premier Six Senses Hideaway du Moyen-Orient ne pouvait pas être plus spectaculaire ! Les 80 villas ont été construites dans le style traditionnel d'Oman. L'aménagement intérieur est inspiré de la culture arabe, fuyant cependant de tout apparat ostentatoire. Le programme de gestion environnementale détaillé surveille l'impact contrôlé sur l'environnement.

Zighy Bay, en la punta norte de la Península de Musandam, tiene por un lado los agrietados acantilados de las montañas de Hadschar y por el otro una playa de arena de 1,6 kilómetros de longitud: la situación del primer Six Senses Hideaway en Oriente Medio no podía ser mejor. Las 82 villas están construidas en el estilo tradicional de Omán. El diseño interior está inspirado en la cultura árabe, renunciando a todo tipo de pompa supérflua. El detallado „Environment Management Program" (Programa de Gestión Medioambiental), se encarga del respeto al medio ambiente.

Su di un lato le rocce frastagliate del monte Hadschar con le sue profonde vallate, sull'altro i 1,6 chilometrei di spiaggia di sabbia della Zighy Bay, all'estremità settentrionale della penisola di Musandam; non poteva esserci posto migliore per il primo Six Senses Hideaway, in Medioriente. Le sue 82 ville sono state costruite nello stile tradizionale dell'Oman. Il design degli interni si ispira alla cultura araba pur rinunciando allo sfarzo troppo evidente. Un dettagliato „Environment Management Program" garantisce il rispetto per l'ambiente.

The 247 square metre villas offer every comfort imaginable and personal butler service.

Die mindestens 247 Quadratmeter großen Villen bieten jeden erdenklichen Komfort und einen persönlichen Butlerservice.

Ces villas d'une surface minimale de 247 m² proposent toutes les commodités imaginables ainsi que les services d'un majordome personnel!

Las grandes villas, de la menos 247 m², ofrecen todas las comodidades imaginables y un servicio de mayordomo personal.

Le ville sono grandi almeno 247 metri quadri ed offrono tutti i conforts immaginabili, compreso un servizio di maggiordomo personale.

Greystoke Mahale

Lake Tanganyika, Tanzania

Sometimes tourism can save lives - even the lives of chimpanzees. Poachers were on their way to wiping out the entire population of apes when the Greystoke Mahale opened the nature reserve and prohibited hunting. Since then the six bandas (as the traditional thatched roof huts are called) have accommodated guests from all over the world travelling to Tanzania's Lake Tanganyika to observe the apes on extended walking-tours. The furniture in the spacious huts is made from dhows, old Arabian sailing vessels. The top floor of the bandas are reached by ladders fashioned from dugout canoes.

Manchmal kann Tourismus Leben retten - und wenn es das von Schimpansen ist. Wilderer waren auf dem besten Weg, die gesamte Population der Menschenaffen auszurotten, als das Greystoke Mahale das Naturreservat touristisch erschloss und die Jagd verhinderte. Die sechs Bandas, wie die traditionellen schilfgedeckten Hütten heißen, beherbergen seither Gäste aus aller Welt, die an Tanzanias Tanganyika See reisen, um auf ausgedehnten Wanderungen die Menschenaffen zu beobachten. Die Möbel in den großzügigen Hütten sind aus Dhows gefertigt, den alten arabischen Segelbooten. Über Leitern aus Einbäumen erreicht man das obere Stockwerk der Bandas.

Le tourisme peut quelquefois sauver des vies, même lorsqu'il s'agit de celles des chimpanzés. Les chasseurs furtifs étaient en train de décimer la population des anthropoïdes, lorsque la réserve naturelle du Greystoke Mahale a ouvert ses portes au tourisme et a interdit la chasse. Les six « bandas », comment sont dénommées ces huttes traditionnelles couvertes de roseaux, abritent depuis lors des clients venus du monde entier pour découvrir le lac Tanganyka de Tanzanie et observer les chimpanzés lors d'excursión. Les meubles de ces cabanes aux dimensions généreuses sont construits en dhows, ces anciens voiliers arabes. Des échelles confectionnées à partir de pirogues permettent d'arriver aux étages supérieurs des bandas.

A veces, el turismo puede salvar vidas, aunque sea la de los chimpancés. Los animales salvajes estaban a punto de ser exterminados cuando Greystoke Mahale desarrolló turísticamente la reserva natural y prohibió la caza. Las seis Bandas, como se denominan las cabañas tradicionales cubiertas con juncos, alojan desde entonces a visitantes de todo el Mundo que visitan el Lago Tanganica en Tanzania para observar a los chimpancés en largos excursións. Los muebles de las amplias cabañas están fabricados con dhow, las antiguas embarcaciones a vela árabes. Mediante escaleras de mano hechas con cayucos se llega al piso superior de las Bandas.

Talvolta il turismo può salvare delle vite – anche quelle degli scimpanzè. Alcuni bracconieri erano quasi riusciti a sterminare l'intera popolazione delle scimmie, quando il Greystoke Mahale aprì al turismo la riserva naturale ed impedì la caccia. Da allora le sei bandas, come vengono chiamate le tradizionali capanne dal tetto di canne, ospitano turisti di tutto il mondo che giungono in Tanzania, al lago Tanganyika, per osservare le scimmie durante lunghi safari. I mobili delle splendide capanne sono fabbricati con i dhows, le antiche imbarcazioni arabe. Le scale fabbricate con il legno delle piroghe portano al piano superiore delle bandas.

The textiles in the bandas originate from local weaving mills.

Die Textilien in den Bandas stammen aus heimischen Webereien, die Handwerkskunst wurde in der Region gefertigt.

Les étoffes utilisées dans les bandas proviennent des tissages autochtones et l'artisanat provient de la propre région.

Las telas de las Bandas proceden de telares locales, artesanía producida en la región.

Tutti i prodotti tessili delle bandas sono prodotti in fabbriche di tessuti del posto, i prodotti artistici artigianali provengono dalla regione.

Greystoke Mahale *Lake Tanganyika, Tanzania*   85

Xaranna Okavango Delta Camp

Okavango Delta, Botswana

A 25.000 hectare nature reserve in the middle of the Okavango Delta surrounds the Xaranna Okovango Delta Camp in Botswana. The distinctive landscape is shaped by thousands of meandering waters constantly changing their course. The nine luxuriously furnished tents in the camp can only be reached by boat. There are diverse measures to protect this valuable ecosystem; from the release of endangered species facing extinction back into the wild such as black rhinos to the protection of the dying tropical forest.

Ein Naturreservat von 25 000 Hektar mitten im Okavango Delta umgibt das Xaranna Okovango Delta Camp in Botswana. Tausende von mäandernden Wasseradern, die ihren Lauf ständig verändern, prägen die eigentümliche Landschaft. Die neun luxuriös ausgestatteten Zelte des Camps sind nur mit dem Boot erreichbar. Vielfältig sind die Maßnahmen, dieses wertvolle Ökosystem zu bewahren. Von der Auswilderung vom Aussterben bedrohter Tierarten wie des Schwarzen Rhinos bis zum Schutz des gefährdeten Tropenwalds.

Une réserve naturelle de 25000ha, située en plein cœur du delta de Okavango, entoure le Xaranna Okovango Delta Camp de Botswana. Les méandres des milliers de veines d'eau, modifiant sans cesse leur tracé, parcourent le paysage caractéristique. Les neuf tentes du campement, à l'aménagement luxueux, ne peuvent être atteintes qu'en bateau. Diverses mesures protègent ce précieux écosystème. Depuis la protection des espèces animales en danger d'extinction par le fait des braconniers, comme le rhinocéros noir, jusqu'à la protection de la forêt tropicale menacée.

Una reserva natural de 25.000 hectáreas en medio del Delta del Okavango, rodea al Xaranna Okovango Delta Camp de Botswana. Este paisaje único está salpicado de miles de norias que cambian constantemente de sentido. Las nueve tiendas del Campamento, lujosamente decoradas, sólo tienen acceso en barco. Para preservar este ecosistema se toman numerosas medidas: desde la reintroducción de especies animales en peligro de extinción, como el rinoceronte negro, hasta la protección de la amenazada selva tropical.

Una riserva naturale di 25000 ettari nel cuore del delta dell'Okavango circonda lo Xaranna Okovango Delta Camp in Botswana. Migliaia di rivoli d'acqua che modificano continuamente il loro corso, formando profondi meandri, sono la caratteristica di questo singolare paesaggio. Le nove tende del campo, arredate con lusso, possono essere raggiunte solo con un battello. Molteplici sono le iniziative che tentano di conservare questo prezioso ecosistema. Si tenta di rinselvatichire specie animali in via di estinzione, come il rinoceronte nero, e di proteggere la Sand Forest, anch'essa a rischio di estinzione.

The interior design of the camp shows a contemporary, urban inspired safari style.

Einen zeitgemäßen, urban inspirierten Safari-Stil zeigt das Interior Design des Camps.

Un style safari, contemporain et d'inspiration urbaine, marque le design et l'aménagement intérieur du campement.

El diseño de interior del campamento está inspirado en un moderno y urbano estilo Safari.

Uno stile safari contemporaneo e di ispirazione urbana caratterizza il design degli interni del campo.

Xaranna Okavango Delta Camp *Okavango Delta, Botswana*

North Island

North Island, Seychelles

4° 22' South, 55° 13' East—coordinates worth noting. That's because the resort on this small island gives rise to visions of heavenly climes. Nestled in the greenery of the trees, ten of the eleven villas comprise over 4800-square feet. There, every conceivable comfort together with private refreshing pool, designer furniture, and a lawn in front of the terrace await. Yet, the lodge presents itself as environmentally-friendly and original: in half African, half Balinese style.

4° 22' Süd, 55° 13' Ost – eine Positionsbestimmung zum Vormerken. Denn das Resort dieses kleinen Eilandes lässt Erinnerungen an paradiesische Zustände aufkommen. Versteckt im Grün der Bäume, bieten zehn der elf Villen 450 m², die neu ausgebaute elfte sogar 750 m². Darin wartet jeglicher Komfort mit eigenem Erfrischungspool, Designermöbeln und Liegewiese vor der Terrasse. Gleichwohl präsentiert sich die Lodge umweltschonend und ursprünglich: im Stil halb afrikanisch, halb balinesisch.

4° 22' Sud, 55° 13' Est – une position dont on doit se souvenir. En effet, le domaine de cette petite île réveille des souvenirs de conditions paradisiaques. Cachées dans le vert des arbres, dix des onze villas possèdent une superficie de 450 m². Là vous attend un confort complet et une piscine privée pour vous rafraîchir, des meubles de designers et une pelouse de détente devant la terrasse. Le pavillon a une apparence naturelle et originelle : de style moitié africain, moitié balinais.

4° 22' Sur, 55° 13' Este –una posición a tener en cuenta, ya que el resort en esta pequeña isla evoca sensaciones paradisíacas. Escondidos tras el verde de los árboles, diez de los once villas tienen 450 m². Aquí se encuentran todo tipo de comodidades: Una piscina propia, muebles de diseño y un prado para tumbarse delante de la terraza. No obstante, el diseño es auténtico y compatible con el medio ambiente: Un estilo mitad africano, mitad balinés.

4° 22' sud, 55° 13' est: una posizione da ricordare. Il resort di questa piccola isola rammenta, non a caso, il paradiso. Nascoste nel verde degli alberi, dieci delle undici ville han un'area di 450 m². Al loro interno si trova ogni genere di confort: una piscina per rinfrescarsi, mobili di design e un solarium davanti alla terrazza. Allo stesso tempo il lodge rispetta l'ambiente con la sua originalità: uno stile misto tra l'africano ed il balinese.

Living like Robinson Crusoe without having to sacrifice western luxury—that's the special charm of North Island.

Leben wie Robinson Crusoe ohne auf westlichen Luxus verzichten zu müssen – darin liegt der besondere Reiz von North Island.

Vivre comme Robinson Crusoé, sans renoncer cependant au luxe occidental – c'est le défi relevé par North Island.

Vivir como Robinson Crusoe sin tener que renunciar al lujo occidental, eso es lo que hace especialmente atractiva la North Island.

Vivere come Robinson Crusoe senza dover rinunciare al lusso occidentale: è questo il fascino particolare della North Island.

Constance Lodge Tsarabanjina

Tsarabanjina Island, Madagascar

Located on a small island in the middle of the Indian Ocean off the coast of Madagascar, lined with powdery white sandy beaches. Gentle breaking waves and the singing of birds provide the background music for the 25 thatched-roof guest bungalows. There is no television or telephone available. The island is shared with the smallest chameleon in the world. The tropical paradise has preserved a variety of species requiring protection. This was the aim of the Constance Lodge on Tsarabanjina Island.

Ein kleines Eiland inmitten des Indischen Ozeans vor der Küste Madagaskars. Gesäumt von puderig weißen Sandstränden. Sanft anrollende Wellen und der Gesang der Vögel liefern die Hintergrundmusik für die 25 strohgedeckten Gästebungalows. Es gibt kein Fernsehen und kein Telefon. Dafür teilt man die Insel mit dem kleinsten Chamäleon der Welt. Das tropische Paradies hat sich eine Artenvielfalt bewahrt, die es zu schützen gilt. Diesem Ziel hat sich die Constance Lodge auf Tsarabanjinas mit vielfältigen Programmen verpflichtet.

Une petite île en plein milieu de l'océan Indien, devant les côtes de Madagascar. Entourée de plages de sable blanc et fin. Les vagues s'échouent paresseusement sur le littoral et le chant des oiseaux assure l'animation musicale pour les 25 bungalows recouverts de paille et destinés aux clients. Il n'y a ni téléviseur, ni téléphone. En contrepartie, le client partage l'île avec le plus petit caméléon du monde. Ce paradis tropical a réussi à conserver la diversité des espèces dont la protection doit être assurée aujourd'hui. Voilà l'objectif que s'est fixé le Constance Lodge de Tsarabanjinas, sur la base d'un programme très varié.

Un pequeño islote en medio del Océano Índico, ante la costa de Madagascar. Rodeado de playas de finísima arena blanca. Olas que envuelven suavemente y el canto de las aves proporcionan la música de fondo de los 25 bungalows con techo de paja. No hay televisión ni teléfono. Pero hay que compartir la isla con el camaleón más pequeño del Mundo. El paraíso tropical se ha conservado de múltiples maneras. Con este objetivo, el Constance Lodge de Tsarabanjinas se ha comprometido con diversos programas.

Una piccola isola nel bel mezzo dell'Oceano Indiano, davanti alle coste del Madagascar. Limitata da spiagge di sabbia bianca sottile come cipria. Il dolce sciabordio delle onde ed il canto degli uccelli fanno da melodioso sottofondo nei 25 bungalows dal tetto di paglia. Non ci sono televisori, ne' telefoni. Sull'isola vive anche il più piccolo camaleonte del mondo. Questo paradiso tropicale è riuscito a conservare una varietà di specie che ora bisogna proteggere. Questo è l'obiettivo che con diversi programmi si propone di realizzare il Constance Lodge sull'isola di Tsarabanjinas.

You can travel lightly and arrive at the barefoot resort with no more than a swimsuit and a t-shirt.

Mit kleinem Gepäck kann man in das Barfuß-Resort anreisen, Badeanzug und T-Shirt genügen.

L'équipage pour voyager dans ce complexe hôtelier de l'agence est très simple. Un maillot de bain et un tee-shirt suffisent!

Se puede viajar al resort descalzo con un pequeño equipaje: basta con un bañador y una camiseta.

Non occorre un grande bagaglio per arrivare in questo resort: si può camminare a piedi nudi e come abbigliamento bastano un costume da bagno ed una t-shirt.

98   Constance Lodge Tsarabanjina   *Tsarabanjina Island, Madagascar*

Benguerra Lodge

Benguerra Island, Mozambique

Benguerra Island is part of the Bazaruto Archipelago, one of the very few national marine parks in the world. Strict requirements are imposed on tourism. Guests to the lodge (situated on a blinding white sandy beach) are accompanied during snorkelling and diving in order to ensure protection of the fragile coral reef. Tourists also assume social responsibility, as social projects such as primary school and hospitals are financed by part of the overnight rate.

Benguerra Island gehört zum Bazaruto Archipel, einem der ganz wenigen Meeres-Nationalparks weltweit. Entsprechend streng sind die Auflagen für den Tourismus. Gäste der am blendend weißen Sandstrand gelegenen Lodge werden zum Schnorcheln und Tauchen begleitet, um den Schutz des fragilen Korallenriffs zu gewährleisten. Touristen übernehmen auch soziale Verantwortung: Mit einem Teil der Übernachtungspreise werden soziale Projekte auf der Insel finanziert, wie die Grundschule oder die Krankenstation.

Benguerra Island fait partie de l'archipel de Bazaruto, l'un des rares parcs naturels marins du monde. Les conditions appliquées au tourisme y seront sévères. Les vacanciers souhaitant faire de la plongée au tuba sont accompagnés à la plage de sable blanc étincelant, situé près du complexe, dans le but d'assurer la protection de la délicate barrière de corail. Les clients assument aussi une responsabilité sociale : une partie du prix des nuitées est consacrée au financement de projets sociaux de l'île, comme l'école primaire ou l'infirmerie, par exemple.

La Isla Benguerra pertenece al Archipiélago Bazaruto, uno de los poquísimos parques nacionales marítimos del Mundo, y de ahí los estrictos cupos turísticos. Se acompaña a los huéspedes de los alojamientos, situados en la blancas playas de arena, a bucear a pulmón y a hacer submarinismo para garantizar la protección de los frágiles arrecifes de coral. Los turistas asumen también responsabilidades sociales: con parte del precio del alojamiento se financian proyectos sociales en la isla, como el colegio o el hospital.

L'isola di Benguerra fa parte dell'arcipelago Bazaruto, uno degli ormai pochi parchi nazionali marini nel mondo. Per questo motivo sull'isola vigono obblighi severi per il turista. Gli ospiti del lodge, che si trova su una spiaggia di sabbia bianca abbagliante, vengono accompagnati nelle immersioni in mare per controllare e garantire la protezione della delicata barriera corallina. I turisti si assumono anche una responsabilità sociale: con una parte dei costi per il pernottamento vengono finanziati progetti sociali sull'isola, quali la scuola elementare o l'ambulatorio medico.

The traditional reed-covered cabanas and villas are designed in the enticing colonial safari style.

Die traditionell reetgedeckten Cabanas und Villen sind im einladenden kolonialen Safari-Stil gestaltet.

Les cabanes et les villas recouvertes de paille à la manière traditionnelle sont construites dans un agréable style safari colonial.

Las cabañas cubiertas con juncos y las villas están decoradas en un acogedor estilo colonial de safari.

Così come le ville anche le grandi cabanas, dal tetto ricoperto di canne come da tradizione, sono arredate secondo l'affascinante stile safari del periodo coloniale.

Okahirongo Elephant Lodge

Kaokoland, Namibia

For a long time travellers to Namibia only experienced the legendary Kaokoveld (land of Himbas) by jeep. Now guests can stay there and enjoy the unique beauty of this wild and unspoilt landscape. A maximum of 18 guests can stay overnight in the comfortable chalets at the Okahirongo Elephant Lodge and on game drives observe giraffes, desert elephants, black rhinos, and lions in their natural surroundings. As a logistics center for research the lodge is extensively involved in a project for desert lions.

Lange haben Namibia-Reisende das legendäre Kaokoveld, Land der Himbas, nur vom Jeep aus erlebt. Nun kann man dort bleiben und die einzigartige Schönheit dieser wilden und unberührten Landschaft genießen. Maximal 18 Gäste können in den komfortablen Chalets der Okahirongo Elephant Lodge übernachten und bei Pirschfahrten Giraffen, Wüstenelefanten, schwarze Nashörner und Löwen in ihrer natürlichen Umgebung beobachten. Als Logistikzentrum für Forscher ist die Lodge maßgeblich an einem Forschungsprojekt zum Leben der Wüstenlöwen beteiligt.

Pendant très longtemps les voyageurs vers la Namibie n'ont connu le légendaire Kaokoveld, le pays des Himbas, que depuis leur jeep. L'on peut maintenant y séjourner et profiter de l'incroyable beauté de ses parages sauvages intacts. Un maximum de 18 visiteurs peuvent séjourner dans les chalets confortables de l'Okahirongo Elephant Lodge et observer au cours de safari-photo, et dans leur habitat naturel, les girafes, les chameaux, les rhinocéros noirs et les lions. En tant que centre logistique destiné aux chercheurs, ce complexe résidentiel participe également à un projet de recherche sur la vie des lions du désert.

Durante mucho tiempo, el viajero por Namibia al legendario Desierto de Kaoko, tierra de los Himbas, sólo podía experimentarlo en Jeep. Ahora se puede permanecer allí y disfrutar de la belleza única de este paisaje natural intacto. Un máximo de 18 huéspedes se pueden alojar en los cómodos chalets de Okahirongo Elephant Lodge y contemplar en safaris fotográficos jirafas, elefantes del desierto, rinocerontes negros y leones en su entorno natural. El centro participa decisivamente en un proyecto de investigación de la vida de los leones del desierto como centro logístico para investigadores.

Per molti anni gli escursionisti della Namibia hanno potuto conoscere la leggendaria Kaokoveld, terra degli Himbas, solo a bordo della loro jeep. Oggi possono anche fermarsi qui e godere della singolare bellezza di questo paesaggio selvaggio ed intatto. Non più di 18 ospiti possono pernottare nei confortevoli chalets dell'Okahirongo Elephant Lodge e durante i safari possono osservare giraffe, elefanti, rinoceronti neri e leoni nel loro habitat naturale. Essendo un importante centro logistico per esploratori il lodge è stato inserito in un progetto di ricerca sulla vita dei leoni.

The individual lodge design with its amorphous shapes places strong emphasis on the wild landscape.

Die eigenwillige Bauweise der Lodge mit ihren amorphen Formen setzt einen starken Akzent in der wilden Landschaft.

Le style de construction du Lodge, réalisé volontairement en formes amorphes, s'adapte formidablement à ce paysage sauvage.

La original forma de construcción del alojamiento, con sus formas amorfas, pone un fuerte acento en el paisaje salvaje.

L'originale costruzione del lodge con le sue linee senza una forma definita spicca in modo deciso nel paesaggio selvaggio.

Boulders Safari Camp

Wolwedans, NamibRand Nature Reserve, Namibia

The camp lies in the middle of the NamibRand Nature Reserve, former farmland that has been renaturalized. Farm animals have been relocated and fences torn down in order to return the wildlife to their natural living space, that they must now share with camp guests. Every guest can enjoy two million square metres of pure wilderness. The four tents have been built according to ecological criteria without encroaching on nature. The interior cultivates a contemporary safari chic.

Das Camp liegt inmitten des NamibRand Naturreservats, früheres Farmland, das renaturiert wurde. Nutztiere wurden umgesiedelt, Zäune niedergerissen, um den Wildtieren, Hyänen und Leoparden, ihren natürlichen Bewegungsraum zurück zu geben, den sie mit maximal acht Gästen des Camps teilen müssen. Dabei kommt auf jeden Gast eine Fläche von zwei Millionen Quadratmeter pure Wildnis. Die vier Zelte wurden nach ökologischen Gesichtspunkten errichtet, ohne bautechnische Eingriffe in die Natur. Das Interieur kultiviert einen zeitgemäßen Safari-Chic.

Le campement est situé au beau milieu de la réserve naturelle du NamibRand, une ancienne terre cultivée qui a été dévolue à son état naturel. Les animaux domestiques ont été déplacés, les clôtures arrachées, pour rendre aux animaux sauvages, comme les hyènes et les léopards, leurs espaces naturels qu'ils devront partager avec un maximum de huit visiteurs de ce campement. Chacun des clients dispose d'une superficie de 2 millions de mètres carrés de pur territoire sauvage! Les quatre tentes ont été construites dans le respect des règles écologiques et sans que la construction ne cause d'impact sur la nature. L'aménagement intérieur est moderne, dans le style safari.

El campamento se sitúa en medio de la reserva natural NamibRand, que era antiguamente una granja que ha sido devuelta a la naturaleza. Los animales de granja han sido devueltos a la naturaleza y las vallas han sido abatidas para devolver a los animales salvajes, hienes y leopardos, su espacio de movimiento natural, ya que en el campamento se aloja a un máximo de ocho clientes. A cada huesped le corresponde una superficie de dos millones de metros cuadrados de región salvaje. Las cuatro tiendas de campaña se han construido desde un punto de vista ecológico, sin el uso de técnicas de construcción perjudiciales para la naturaleza. El interior goza de un moderno estilo safari elegante.

Il campo si trova nel mezzo della riserva naturale di NamibRand, un tempo territorio adibito a fattoria che poi è stato nuovamente naturalizzato. Gli animali da lavoro sono stati trasferiti e i recinti abbattuti per restituire agli animali selvaggi, iene e leopardi, il loro spazio naturale, che oggi condividono con gli ospiti del campo (massimo 8 persone). Così ciascun ospite ha a disposizione una superficie di 2 milioni di metri quadrati di pura natura selvaggia. Le quattro tende sono state allestite seguendo criteri ecologici, senza alterare la natura con interventi tecnologici o edilizi. Gli interni si ispirano ad un moderno stile safari.

The infinite expanse can become a spiritual experience.

Die Erfahrung von unendlicher Weite kann zum spirituellen Erlebnis werden.

L'expérience des étendues sans fin peut devenir une aventure spirituelle.

La experiencia de una extensión ilimitada se puede convertir en una vivencia espiritual.

L'esperienza degli spazi sconfinati può trasformarsi in esperienza spirituale.

Grootbos Forest Lodge

Hermanus, South Africa

Floor to ceiling glazed windows of the lobby at Forest Lodge provide a magnificent view of Walker Bay – the south African Eldorado for whale watching. The lodge with its 16 luxury suites is set in a 1750 hectare nature reserve. Merely to build in an ecological way was not enough for owner Michael Lutzeyer. He established a foundation with the task of protecting the valuable and exceptionally rich variety of Feynbos flora (unique to the Cape) and to involve guests in this project.

Von den raumhoch verglasten Fensterfronten der Lobby der Forest Lodge eröffnet sich ein weiter Blick über die Walker Bay – das südafrikanische Eldorado zum Wale beobachten. Die Lodge mit ihren 16 Luxussuiten liegt in einem 1750 Hektar großen Naturreservat. Lediglich umweltverträglich zu bauen, war Besitzer Michael Lutzeyer zu wenig. Er gründete gleich eine Stiftung, deren Aufgabe es ist, die wertvolle und ungemein artenreiche Flora des Feynbos, wie die einzigartige Pflanzenwelt am Kap heißt, zu schützen und die Gäste dabei in das Projekt einzubinden.

Depuis les immenses baies vitrées du hall de réception du Forest Lodge, vous découvrirez une vue panoramique sur la Walker Bay, cet eldorado sud-africain pour l'observation des cétacés. Ce lodge de 16 suites de luxes est situé dans une réserve naturelle de 1750ha. Il n'était pas suffisant pour Michael Lutzeyer, le propriétaire, de construire dans le respect de l'environnement et d'éviter les pollutions. Il lui fallait aussi créer une fondation dont la tâche est de protéger la précieuse et diverse flore de Feynbos, comme est dénommé le monde des plantes au Cap, unique en son genre. Il souhaitait également inclure les clients dans ce projet.

A través de las vidrieras del vestíbulo del Forest Lodge se abre un amplio panorama de la Bahía de Walker, el Eldorado sudafricano para avistar ballenas. El hotel con sus 16 lujosas suites está situado en una reserva natural de 1750 hectáreas. Al propietario Michael Lutzeyer no le bastaba únicamente con construirlo cuidando el medio ambiente. Al mismo tiempo creó una fundación para proteger la valiosa e increiblemente extensa flora de Fynbos, como se denomina la formación vegetal endémica de la región del Cabo, e implicar a los visitantes en el proyecto.

Dalle alte vetrate del salone del Forest Lodge si apre un'ampia veduta sulla Walker Bay – eletta all'unanimità Eldorado del Sud Africa. Il lodge comprende 16 suites di lusso e si trova in una riserva naturale di 1750 ettari. Il proprietario Michael Lutzeyer non solo ha provveduto a costruire gli edifici riducendo al minimo l'impatto ambientale, ma ha anche dato vita ad una fondazione che si ripromette di tutelare la preziosa flora del Feynbo, come viene chiamato il mondo vegetale nel promontorio, straordinariamente ricca di specie naturali. Allo stesso modo si impegna anche a coinvolgere gli ospiti nel progetto.

Sand and mudstone with slight orange coloured accents give the rooms a contemporary comfort.

Sand- und Schlammtöne mit wenigen orangefarbenen Akzenten verleihen den Räumen eine zeitgemäße Behaglichkeit.

Des coloris sable et argile, avec peu de tons orangés, donnent aux murs une teinte chaleureuse et moderne.

Toneladas de barro y arena con cierto tono anaranjado, proporcionan a los espacios un ambiente moderno.

Le sfumature dei colori della sabbia e del fango, insieme ad alcuni toni arancio rendono gli ambienti moderni ed accoglienti.

El Capitan Canyon

Santa Barbara, California, USA

Back to the simple things that really make people happy. This is what El Capitan Canyon Lodge on the Californian coast wants to bring to every guest: sinking into a crystal-clear starry sky at night, hiking miles of trails through the foothills, and sitting by a blazing open fire in the evening. Simple cedar cabins or safari tents accommodate guests. Solar energy is used to power lights and heat the pool. For trees that have been uprooted by winter storms there is a rescue programme that saves them from ending up as firewood. Instead, the lodge workshop reserves the wood for other uses.

Zurück zu den einfachen Dingen, die Menschen wirklich glücklich machen, will die El Capitan Canyon Lodge an der kalifornischen Küste ihre Gäste bringen. Nachts in einen glasklaren Sternenhimmel versinken, kilometerweit durch das Gebirge wandern, abends beim lodernden Feuer sitzen. Man wohnt in einfachen Zedernhütten oder Safarizelten. Solarzellen liefern Energie für die Beleuchtung und beheizen den Pool. Für Bäume, die etwa Winterstürme entwurzelten, gibt es ein Rettungsprogramm, das sie davor bewahrt als Feuerholz zu enden: Im Workshop der Lodge wird ihr Holz zu nützlichen Dingen verarbeitet.

El Capitan Canyon Lodge, situé sur la côte californienne, veut revenir vers les choses simples, celles qui rendent les gens véritablement heureux. Se fondre la nuit dans un ciel étoilé clair et transparent, s'installer le soir venu devant une flambée dans la cheminée. L'habitat est constitué de simples cabanes en bois de cèdre ou des tentes de safari. 75% de l'énergie est produite par des panneaux solaires. Les arbres déracinés par des tempêtes bénéficient d'un programme de sauvetage qui leur évite de terminer en bois de cheminée: l'atelier du lodge transforme ce bois en objets utiles.

El Capitan Canyon Lodge, en la costa de California, quiere que sus huéspedes vuelvan a las cosas sencillas, las que hacen a las personas realmente felices. Hundirse en un transparente cielo estrellado, sentándose por la noche alrededor de un cálido fuego. Se vive en sencillas cabañas de cedro o tiendas de campaña tipo safari. El 75% de la energía procede de células solares. Existe un programa para la salvación de árboles arrancados por las tormentas invernales, que antes habrían acabado en el fuego: en el workshop del alojamiento se transformará la madera en objetos útiles.

Ricondurre l'uomo alle piccole cose che lo rendono veramente felice: questo è l'obiettivo del El Capitan Canyon Lodge sulla costa della California. Ammirare di notte un limpido cielo stellato, sedersi di sera accanto ad un fuoco scoppiettante. Gli ospiti alloggiano in semplici capanne di legno di cedro o in tende da safari. Il 75% dell'energia adoperata proviene da celle solari. E' attualmente in corso un progetto elaborato per salvare gli alberi che in inverno venivano sradicati dalle tempeste di vento e per evitare che si utilizzassero come legna da ardere. Nella bottega del lodge con il loro legno si producono oggetti utili.

The El Capitan Canyon Nature Lodge on the Californian coast north of Santa Barbara seeks to be an alternative to everything that is artificial in appearance.

Ein Gegenentwurf zu allem nur Äußerlichen und Gekünstelten will die El Capitan Canyon Nature Lodge an der kalifonischen Küste nördlich von Santa Barbara sein.

Contrairement à tout ce qui ne mise que sur l'apparence et le côté factice des choses, El Capitan veut être le canyon nature Lodge du littoral californien, au nord de Santa Barbara.

El Capitan Canyon Nature Lodge en la costa californiana al norte de Santa Barbara quiere mantenerse alejado de todo lo superfluo y artificial.

Il lodge El Capitan Canyon Nature sulla costa californiana a nord di Santa Barbara vuole essere una proposta contro tutto ciò che consiste solo di esteriorità e di ricercatezza.

120   El Capitan Canyon *Santa Barbara, California, USA*

Amangani

Jackson, Wyoming, USA

The architecture of the luxury hotel, awarded with numerous prizes, reflects the raw unspoilt landscape in Wyoming. The elongated three-storey-high building is nestled into the grounds; its hipped roof carries the outline of the characteristic rocky landscape. Covered with cedar wood shingles it almost looks like a rocky cliff. From the pool you get a fantastic view of the Rocky Mountains and the Snake River. Local building materials, natural stone from Oklahoma and cedar wood were used in its construction.

Die Architektur des mit zahlreichen Preisen ausgezeichneten Luxushotels reflektiert die raue unverfälschte Landschaft Wyomings. Das langgestreckte, drei Stockwerke hohe Gebäude duckt sich in das Gelände, sein Walmdach nimmt die Umrisse der charakteristischen Felsenlandschaft auf. Eingedeckt mit Zedernholzschindeln wirkt es fast wie ein Felsvorsprung. Vom Pool aus eröffnet sich ein fantastischer Blick auf die Rocky Mountains und den Snake River. Gebaut wurde mit heimischen Materialien, mit Naturstein aus Oklahoma und Zedernholz.

L'architecture de cet hôtel de luxe a été récompensée par de nombreux prix. Elle est le reflet du paysage rude et authentique du Wyoming. Ce bâtiment de trois étages, construit tout en hauteur, se niche dans le paysage. Son toit en croupe adopte les contours caractéristiques du paysage rocheux des alentours. Couvert par des bardeaux en bois de cèdre, il ressemble presque à une avancée rocheuse. Depuis la piscine, vous bénéficiez d'une formidable vue panoramique sur les Rocky Mountains et le Snake River. La construction s'est faite avec des matériaux autochtones, des pierres naturelles en provenance d'Oklahoma et du bois de cèdre.

La arquitectura de este extraordinario hotel de lujo, que cuenta con numerosos premios, refleja el áspero y genuino paisaje de Wyoming. El amplio edificio de tres plantas de altura se adapta al terreno, su tejado a cuatro aguas acomoda el contorno del característico paisaje rocoso. Cubierto con tablillas de madera de centro parece casi un saliente rocoso. Desde la piscina hay una fantástica vista de las Montañas Rocosas y del río Snake. Está construido con materiales naturales, con piedra natural de Oklahoma y madera de cedro.

L'architettura di questo hotel di lusso, insignito di numerosi premi, riflette il rustico paesaggio naturale del Wyoming. Il lungo edificio, alto tre piani digrada verso il terreno, il suo tetto a padiglione riprende i tratti del caratteristico paesaggio roccioso. Ricoperto di scandole di legno di cedro sembra quasi uno spuntone di roccia. Dalla piscina si può ammirare il fantastico panorama delle Rocky Mountains e dello Snake River. Il lodge è stato costruito con materiali locali, con pietra dell'Oklahoma e legno di cedro.

Noble simplicity dominates modest yet luxuriously furnished rooms.

Edle Einfachheit dominiert in den zurückhaltend, aber dennoch luxuriös eingerichteten Räumen.

L'élégante simplicité domine dans l'aménagement discret, mais cependant luxueux des espaces intérieurs.

Una noble simplicidad domina en las habitaciones, decoradas discreta y lujosamente.

Si potrebbe definire preziosa semplicità quella dello stile degli ambienti, discreti e comunque lussuosi.

Anse Chastanet

St. Lucia, Caribbean

Trees are allowed to grow through the rooms and glassless windows eliminate the need for air conditioning. With over one hundred steps on steep slopes from the rooms to the beach, there's no need for the gym. The Anse Chastanet on the rocky Southwest coast of St Lucia is one of the pioneers of green tourism. The top suites offer a magnificient view of the two 700 meter steep rock formations rising from the sea that are part of the UNESCO world natural heritage.

Bäume dürfen durch die Räume wachsen, Fenster ohne Glas machen die Air Condition in den 37 Zimmern überflüssig. Die mehr als hundert Treppenstufen von einer der feinsandigen Buchten zu den Zimmern, die in den Steilhang gebaut wurden, ersetzen das Gym. Das Anse Chastanet an der felsigen Südwestküste St. Lucias gehört zu den Pionieren des grünen Tourismus. Von den oberen Suiten eröffnet sich ein grandioser Blick auf die beiden Pitons, die zwei 700 Meter steil aus dem Meer ragenden Felskegel, die zum UNESCO Weltnaturerbe zählen.

Les arbres poussent dans les chambres, les fenêtres sans vitres rendent la climatisation inutile dans les 37 chambres de cet établissement. L'escalier de plus de 100 marches, reliant l'une des criques de sable aux chambres par une pente abrupte, remplace avantageusement la gym. Le Anse Chastanet, situé sur la côte rocheuse du sud-ouest de Sainte-Lucie, fait partie des pionniers du tourisme vert. Une grandiose vue panoramique sur les deux pitons, ces pointes rocheuses, surgissant à 700m de la surface de la mer, sont inscrites au patrimoine mondial de l'Unesco.

Los árboles crecen en las habitaciones y las ventanas sin cristal hacen superfluo el aire acondicionado. Los más de cien escalones de la escalera que conduce de una cala de fina arena a las habitaciones construida en un precipicio hace las veces de gimnasio. El Hotel Anse Chastanet, en la rocosa costa suroeste de St. Lucia es uno de los pioneros del turismo verde. Desde las suites superiores hay una espectacular vista de los dos volcanes Piton, las dos rocas que sobresalen del mar con más de 700 metros, declarados por la UNESCO Patrimonio Natural de la Humanidad.

Gli alberi crescono liberi anche al centro delle stanze, nelle 37 camere non occorre aria condizionata grazie alle finestre senza vetri. I cento e più scalini che portano da un'insenatura di sabbia finissima alle camere costruite lungo il pendio sostituiscono la palestra. L' Anse Chastanet sulla costa rocciosa sud-occidentale di St. Lucia è una delle prime strutture per il turismo verde. Dalle suites più in alto si gode di una grandiosa veduta sui due pitons, i due scogli a forma di cono, alti 700 metri, che si ergono ripidi nel mare, proclamati dall'UNESCO patrimonio naturale dell'umanità.

Many artists such as German Stefan Szczesny find inspiration for their work in the strong Caribbean colors.

Zahlreiche Künstler, wie der Deutsche Stefan Szczesny, ließen sich hier von den starken karibischen Farben zu kraftvollen Kunstwerken inspirieren.

De très nombreux artistes, comme l'Allemand Stefan Szczesny, y ont cherché l'inspiration pour la réalisation de leurs œuvres, guidés par les fortes couleurs des Caraïbes.

Numerosos artistas, como el alemán Stefan Szczesny, se inspiraron aquí con los fuertes colores del Caribe para realizar obras de arte llenas de fuerza.

I forti colori caraibici di questo luogo hanno ispirato numerosi artisti, tra i quali il tedesco Stefan Szczesny, e ritornano nelle loro intense opere d'arte.

130 Anse Chastanet *St. Lucia, Caribbean*

Jungle Bay Resort & Spa

Dominica, Caribbean

The 35 cottages of the eco-resort on Dominica were built in the treetops of the tropic rainforest. The nature experience is beyond comparison as guests can truly feel part of the jungle world. Hummingbirds nesting at eye level and a breeze from the nearby ocean instead of airconditioning, provides the refreshment. The utmost care was taken in construction, and the social responsibility that the Jungle Bay assumed by integrating people on site is just as important. A previously disadvantaged region of the green island has now turned into one of the most prosperous.

In die Baumkronen des tropischen Regenwalds wurden die 35 Cottages des Eco Resorts auf Dominica gebaut. Das Naturerlebnis ist unvergleichlich, Gäste können sich als Teil der Dschungelwelt fühlen. Kolibris nisten auf Augenhöhe, statt der Air Condition sorgt eine Brise vom nahen Ozean für Erfrischung. Schon beim Bau wurde äußerst behutsam vorgegangen, genauso wichtig ist die soziale Verantwortung, die das Jungle Bay durch das Einbinden der Menschen vor Ort übernommen hat: Aus einer benachteiligten Region der grünen Insel wurde so eine der prosperierendsten.

Les 35 maisonnettes de l'Eco Resort de Saint-Domingue ont été installées dans la cime des arbres de la forêt tropicale de l'île. L'expérience en pleine nature est incomparable. Les visiteurs se sentent partie prenante de la jungle. Les colibris nichent à hauteur des yeux et, remplaçant la climatisation, une brise venue de l'océan tout proche assure le rafraîchissement. De nombreuses précautions ont déjà été prises lors de la construction. La responsabilité sociale, tout aussi importante d'ailleurs, a été pleinement assumée par Jungle Bay en incluant les autochtones dans le projet : c'est ainsi que l'une des régions les plus pauvres de cette île verte est devenue l'une des plus prospères.

En el selva tropical de Dominica, coronada por los árboles, se construyeron las 35 cabañas del Resort ecológico. La experiencia natural es incomparable; los huéspedes pueden sentirse parte del mundo selvático. Los colibríes anidan a la altura de los ojos y una brisa del cercano océano refresca en lugar del aire acondicionado. Se procede prudentemente ya antes de la construcción e igualmente importante es la responsabilidad social que ha contraido Jungle Bay mediante la implicación de las personas del lugar, pues la isla verde ha pasado de ser una región deprimida a una próspera.

I 35 cottages di questo eco-resort sull'isola di Dominica sono stati costruiti tra le chiome degli alberi della foresta tropicale. Gli ospiti vivono la natura in modo unico ed incomparabile e possono realmente sentirsi parte della giungla. I colibrì costruiscono il nido davanti ai loro occhi e la brezza del vicino oceano rende superflua l'aria condizionata. Già nella fase di costruzione si è avuto massimo rispetto per l'ambiente; altrettanto importante è la responsabilità sociale che ha accettato il Jungle Bay assumendo nella struttura gli abitanti del luogo. Una delle regioni più svantaggiate dell'isola verde è diventata così una delle più prospere.

Nature plays the main role in this eco-resort between the sea and the jungle.

Die Natur spielt die Hauptrolle im Öko-Resort zwischen Meer und Dschungel.

La nature a un rôle prépondérant dans ce complexe écologique, entre mer et jungle.

En el Resort ecológico, la naturaleza juega el principal papel entre el mar y la jungla.

La natura è predominante in questo eco-resort tra mare e giungla.

Tiamo

Bahamas, Caribbean

Nassau is only a 15 minute flight from Bahamas' capital city and yet Tiamo is still an insider's tip on South Andros. In construction of the resort the impact on nature was as minimal as possible. Workers cleared the construction site for the 11 bungalows using machetes, not machinery. All energy comes from solar panels and the sea breeze and open airy design replaces the need for air conditioning, while white roofs reflect the sun rays. Even water for the private Jacuzzis on the wooden decks is heated by the sun.

Von der Bahamas-Hauptstadt Nassau ist es nur ein 15 Minuten-Flug und doch ist das Tiamo auf South Andros noch immer ein Geheimtipp. Schon beim Bau des Resorts sollten die Eingriffe in die Natur so gering wie möglich sein. Deshalb rodeten Arbeiter mit Macheten die Bauplätze für die 11 Bungalows, nicht Maschinen. Alle Energie kommt von Solarzellen, die Meeresbrise und das offene luftige Design ersetzen die Klimaanlage, weiße Dächer reflektieren die Sonnenstrahlen. Selbst das Wasser für die privaten Jacuzzis auf den Holzdecks wird von der Sonne erwärmt.

Depuis Nassau, la capitale des Bahamas, 15 minutes d'avion à peine vous emmène à Tiamo sur South Andros. C'est d'ailleurs toujours encore un bon plan encore réservé aux initiés! L'impact sur la nature devait déjà être réduit au minimum lors de la construction du complexe. C'est la raison pour laquelle les ouvriers ont nettoyé à coups de machette les surfaces destinées à recevoir les 11 bungalows, au lieu d'utiliser des machines. Toute l'énergie provient des panneaux solaires et la brise de la mer et le design ouvert, souvent très original, remplace la climatisation. Les toits blancs reflètent d'ailleurs les rayons du soleil. Même l'eau destinée aux jacuzzis privés installés sur les pontons en bois est réchauffée par le soleil.

A pesar de estar situada a 15 minutos de avión de Nassau, capital de Bahamas, Tiamo en la isla de South Andros es todavía un recomendación secreta. Ya en la construcción del Resort la naturaleza debe perjudicarse lo menos posible. Por ello los machetes de los trabajadores cortaron los lugares de construcción de los 11 bungalows sin máquinas. Toda la energía proviene de placas sociales, la brisa del mar y el abierto diseño sustituyen al aire acondicionado, los blancos techos reflejan los rayos del sol. Incluso el agua de los Jacuzzis privados en los techos de maderase calienta con el sol.

Tiamo si trova a soli 15 minuti di volo da Nassau, capitale delle Bahamas, e tuttavia è ancora un luogo segreto. Gli interventi dell'uomo nella natura sono stati ridotti al minimo già nella fase di costruzione del resort. Gli spazi per gli 11 bungalows sono stati dissodati dagli operai con il macete e non con le ruspe. Tutta l'energia proviene da celle solari, la brezza marina e gli spazi aperti ed ariosi rendono inutile l'impianto di climatizzazione, i tetti bianchi riflettono i raggi solari. Persino l'acqua per le Jacuzzi private sulle terrazze in legno è riscaldata dal sole.

An exclusive hideaway for discerning "society's recluses". The resort can only be reached by boat.

Exklusiver Zufluchtsort für anspruchsvolle Zivilisationsflüchtlinge: Das Resort ist nur mit dem Boot erreichbar.

C'est un refuge exclusif, destiné à des réfugiés de la civilisation exigeants : le complexe hôtelier ne peut être rejoint qu'en bateau.

Se trata de un refugio exclusivo para exigentes exiliados de la civilización: sólo se puede llegar al Resort en bote.

Rifugio esclusivo per persone esigenti che vogliono evadere dal mondo civile: il resort è raggiungibile solo con battello.

Azulik

Tulum, Mexico

Bathtub troughs have been carved into the rock faces and rustic huts timbered from local wood. There is no electricity, no telephone, no television, nothing to disturb the experience of nature. Guests fall asleep to the murmurs of the surging waves and wake up to the birds chirping. Nature is the main focus in this 15 room eco-resort on Mexico's Riviera Maya. The mysterious cult sites of Maya are only a stone's throw away. The shimmering turquoise Caribbean Sea makes snorkelling tempting.

Badewannentröge wurden in die Felsen gehauen, rustikale Hütten aus heimischen Hölzern gezimmert. Es gibt keinen Strom, kein Telefon, keinen Fernseher. Nichts stört das Erleben der Natur. Man schläft ein mit dem Murmeln der brandenden Wellen, wacht auf mit dem Zwitschern der Vögel. Die Natur darf die Hauptrolle spielen in diesem 15 Zimmer-Öko-Resort an Mexikos Riviera Maya. Die geheimnisvollen Kultstätten der Mayas sind nur einen Steinwurf entfernt. Das türkis schimmernde karibische Meer lädt zum Schnorcheln ein.

Les baignoires ont été ciselées dans les rochers et les cabanes rustiques construites avec des bois autochtones. Il n'y a ni électricité, ni téléphone, ni téléviseur. Rien ne dérange la communion avec la nature. Vous vous endormez avec le murmure du clapotis des vagues et vous vous réveillez avec le gazouillis des oiseaux. La nature a le rôle principal dans ce complexe hôtelier écologique de 15 chambres installées à Riviera Maya au Mexique. Les hauts lieux Mayas ne sont qu'à un jet de pierre de là. La mer des Caraïbes aux reflets turquoise vous invite à la plongée au tuba.

En las rocas se han excavado bañeras y por otro lado con la madera local se han levantado cabañas rústicas. No hay electricidad, ni teléfono, ni televisión. Nada molesta el disfrute de la naturaleza. Se queda dormido con el rumor de las olas rompiendo contra las rocas y despierta con el trino de los pájaros. La naturaleza es el protagonista en estas 15 habitaciones del resort ecológico de la Riviera Maya de México. Las secretas ciudades sagradas de los mayas se encuentran a tan sólo un tiro de piedra. El turquesa del Mar Caribe invita a bucear.

Le vasche da bagno sono state scavate nella roccia, le rustiche capanne sono state costruite con legno locale. Niente energia elettrica, niente telefono, niente televisore. Nulla disturba chi vuole vivere la natura. Ci si addormenta con il rumore della risacca delle onde, ci si sveglia al mattino con il cinguettio degli uccelli. La natura è protagonista assoluto in questo eco-resort di 15 camere sulla Riviera Maya in Messico. I misteriosi insediamenti religiosi dei Maya si trovano nelle vicinanze. L'invitante mare caraibico dai riflessi turchesi invoglia gli ospiti a fare immersioni.

The huts of the eco-resort look like Robinson made them personally.

Die Hütten des Öko-Resorts sehen aus, als ob Robinson persönlich sie gefertigt hätte.

Les cabanes de ce complexe écologique semblent avoir été préparées pour Robinson Crusoé lui-même!

Parece que las cabañas del resort ecológico las haya construido el mismo Robinson.

Le capanne di questo eco-resort sembrano costruite da Robinson in persona.

Pacuare Lodge

Turrialba, Costa Rica

The Pacuare Lodge on the river of the same name is a pioneer of eco-tourism in Costa Rica. The main concern is the protection of the rainforest. Along the river they acquired 260 hectares that was threatened by deforestation. Each of the 19 guest bungalows offers a 360 degree view of the white foaming Pacuare and the rainforest. The newly built bungalow suites are especially comfortable with four-poster beds and polished teak wood floors. In the main lodge a sprawling terrace invites guests to relax.

Zu den Pionieren des Öko-Tourismus in Costa Rica gehört die Pacuare Lodge am gleichnamigen Fluss. Oberstes Anliegen ist den Betreibern der Schutz des Regenwaldes. Entlang des Flusses erwarben sie 260 Hektar, die von der Abholzung bedroht waren. Jeder der 19 Gäste-Bungalows bietet einen 360 Grad–Blick auf den weiß schäumenden Pacuare und den Regenwald. Besonders komfortabel sind die neu gebauten Bungalow-Suiten mit Himmelbetten und polierten Teakholzböden. In der Haupt-Lodge lädt eine ausladende Terrasse zum Entspannen ein.

Le Lodge Pacuare fait partie des pionniers du tourisme écologique de Costa Rica et se trouve situé sur les rives du fleuve éponyme. La protection de la forêt tropicale est la première préoccupation des exploitants. Ils ont acquis 260ha de terrain menacé de déboisement, sur les rives du fleuve. Chacun des 19 bungalows réservés aux visiteurs profite d'une vue panoramique de 360° sur les eaux tumultueuses à l'écume blanchâtre du fleuve Pacuare et sur la forêt tropicale. Les suites des bungalows de nouvelles constructions sont particulièrement confortables. Ils incorporent des lits à ciel et des sols en bois de teck poli. Le lodge principal possède une terrasse en forme de promontoire, idéale pour le repos.

El Pacuare Lodge, a cuyo río debe su nombre, es el pionero del turismo ecológico en Costa Rica. Su principal prioridad es el fomento de la protección de la jungla. A lo largo del río se han ganado 260 hectáreas que estaban amenazadas por la tala. Cada uno de los huéspedes de los 19 bungalows tiene una vista de 360° hacia el Río Pacuare, de blanca espuma, y a la jungla. Especialmente cómodas son las suites-bungalow con camas con columnas y pulidos suelos de madera de teca. En el alojamiento principal hay una terraza que invita a relajarse.

Il Pacuare Lodge, sul fiume omonimo, è una delle prime strutture per eco-turismo in Costa Rica. La massima aspirazione dei proprietari è salvare la foresta tropicale, perciò hanno acquistato 260 ettari di terreno minacciato dalla deforestazione lungo la riva del fiume. I 19 bungalows per gli ospiti offrono una veduta a 360 gradi sulle acque spumeggianti del Pacuare e sulla foresta tropicale. Molto confortevoli sono i nuovi bungalows-suite con letti a baldacchino e pavimenti in teak lucidato. L'ampia terrazza nel lodge principale è il uogo ideale per il relax.

Taking a holiday in the lodge means getting involved in a rainforest adventure.

In der Lodge Ferien machen, bedeutet, sich auf das Abenteuer Regenwald einzulassen.

Les vacances dans le lodge, demande une soif d'aventure de la forêt tropicale.

Estar de vacaciones en este alojamiento conlleva la aventura de la jungla.

Trascorrere le vacanze in questo lodge significa lasciarsi andare all'avventura nella foresta tropicale.

Las Casitas del Colca

Colca Canyon, Peru

It's impossible for a landscape to be more dramatic: The Colca Canyon in South Peru cuts 3267 meters deep through the rugged Andes. The unique ecosystem is habitat for many species including the mighty Condor. The constructors of Casitas del Colca (opened in 2008) minimized the disruption of this habitat as much as possible. The 20 guest houses were built with local materials. Fruits and vegetables are grown in the hotels's gardens, and organic waste is composted and recycled.

Dramatischer kann eine Landschaft nicht sein: 3267 Meter tief schneidet sich der Colca Canyon im Süden Perus durch die zerklüfteten Anden. Das einzigartige Ökosystem gibt zahlreichen Tierarten den Lebensraum, so auch dem machtvollen Condor. Die Eingriffe in die Natur sollten deswegen beim Bau der 2008 eröffneten Casitas del Colca möglichst minimiert werden. Gebaut wurden die 20 Gästehäuser mit Materialien aus der Region, im hoteleigenen Garten werden Früchte und Gemüse angebaut, organischer Abfall wird kompostiert und wiederverwertet.

Le paysage ne peut pas être plus dramatique: le Colca Canyon, dans le sud du Pérou, ouvre une brèche de 3267m de profondeur dans le relief escarpé des Andes. Son écosystème original inclut de nombreuses espèces animales qui y ont leur habitat, comme, par exemple, le puissant condor. L'impact sur la nature devait donc être réduit au strict minimum lors de la construction de ce complexe Casitas del Colca, inauguré en 2008. Les 20 pavillons réservés aux visiteurs ont été construits avec des matériaux de la région et les fruits et les légumes proviennent des jardins et vergers propres de l'hôtel. Les déchets organiques sont recyclés sous forme de compost et réutilisés.

El paisaje no puede ser más dramático: El Cañón del Colca, al sur de Perú, corta los accidentados Andes con una profundidad de 3267 metros. En este ecosistema único numerosas especies animales tiene su habitat, Como el poderoso condor; por ello, para la apertura de Las Casitas del Colca se intentó minimizar el impacto en la naturaleza. Las 20 casas se construyeron con materiales locales, en el jardín se cosechan las frutas y verduras y se hace compost con los residuos orgánicos para su reutilización.

Non esiste un paesaggio più scenografico di questo: nel sud del Perù il canyon del Colca, profondo 3267 metri, taglia letteralmente le montagne delle Ande con il loro profilo frastagliato. Il suo straordinario ecosistema è abitato da numerose specie animali, qui vive anche l'imponente condor. Perciò, quando è iniziata la costruzione del Casitas del Colca, aperto nel 2008, gli interventi nella natura furono necessariamente ridotti al minimo. Le 20 abitazioni per gli ospiti sono state costruite con materiali della regione, negli orti dell'hotel si coltivano frutta e verdura, i rifiuti organici vengono adoperati per il compostaggio e così rivalorizzati.

The rustic-chic rooms invite guests to relax after thrilling and challenging excursions.

Die Räume im rustikalen Chic laden nach den aufwühlenden und fordernden Exkursionen zum Entspannen ein.

Les chambres, aménagées dans un chic rustique, vous invitent au repos après des excursions passionnantes et éreintantes!

Las habitaciones, en elegante estilo rústico, invitan a realizar agradables y excitantes excursiones para relajarse.

Gli ambienti in stile rustico-elegante consentono un perfetto relax dopo escursioni emozionanti e impegnative.

Las Casitas del Colca *Colca Canyon, Peru*   153

Titilaka

Lake Titicaca, Peru

From the outside the hotel building looks plain, grim, and a little off-putting. However, nothing shall upstage the unique landscape. The position could not be more spectacular: on the southern shore of Lake Titicaca, the highest navigable lake in the world. On the horizon the snow-covered peaks of the Andes are visible. Each of the 18 suites offers a unique view of the Peruvian highland and the lake. Electricity comes from renewable energy sources while a sophisticated concept reduces waste.

Von außen betrachtet ist das Hotelgebäude schlicht, streng, wirkt fast abweisend. Nichts soll der einzigartigen Landschaft die Schau stehlen. Und die Lage könnte nicht spektakulärer sein: am Südufer des Titicaca Sees, des höchstgelegenen schiffbaren Sees der Welt. Am Horizont zeichnen sich die schneebedeckten Gipfel der Anden ab. Jede der 18 Suiten bietet eine großartige Aussicht über das peruanische Hochland und den See. Der Strom kommt von erneuerbaren Energiequellen, ein ausgefeiltes Konzept reduziert den Abfall.

Vu depuis l'extérieur, les bâtiments ont un aspect sévère, presque rébarbatif. Rien ne doit déranger le regard dans ce paysage exceptionnel. Et l'emplacement ne pouvait pas être plus spectaculaire : sur la rive méridionale du lac Titicaca, le lac navigable le plus haut du monde! L'horizon est marqué par les cimes enneigées des Andes. Chacune des 18 suites offre une vue panoramique exceptionnelle sur les hautes terres péruviennes et sur le lac. L'électricité est produite à partir de sources énergétiques renouvelables et un concept bien rodé réduit les déchets.

El edificio del hotel, contemplado desde fuera, parece simple, severo, casi ausente. Nada debe robar protagonismo a este paisaje único. Y su situación no podía ser más espectacular: en la orilla sur del Lago Titicaca, el lago navegable más alto del Mundo. En el horizonte se dibijan las cumbres cubiertas de nieve de Los Andes. Cada una de las 18 suites tiene una magnífica vista sobre la meseta peruana y el lago. La electricidad proviene de fuentes de energía renovables y la basura se reduce gracias a un concepto profundamente meditado.

Visto dall'esterno l'edificio è modesto, severo, e sembra poco ospitale. Nulla deve rubare la scena al paesaggio straordinario. Ed il luogo non poteva essere più spettacolare: sulla sponda meridionale del lago Titicaca, il lago navigabile più alto nel mondo. All'orizzonte si stagliano le cime innevate delle Ande. Le 18 suites offrono una vista straordinaria sull'altopiano peruviano e sul lago. La corrente elettrica proviene da fonti di energia rinnovabili, i rifiuti sono ridotti grazie ad un adeguato programma.

The dream view of the lake is there for all to take in. Lake Titicaca is at risk of silting up with climate change.

Den Traumblick auf den See sollte man tief in sich aufnehmen: Der Titicaca See ist durch den Klimawandel vom Versanden bedroht.

Ne manquez pas d'observer attentivement la merveilleuse vue offerte sur le lac: car le lac Titicaca est menacé d'assèchement par le changement climatique.

Deberiámos grabarnos la magnífica vista, pues el Titicaca esta amenazado de colmatación por el cambio climático.

L'eccezionale veduta sul lago deve essere custodita gelosamente dai turisti: a causa dei mutamenti climatici, infatti, il lago Titicaca rischia di prosciugarsi per l'avanzare della sabbia.

Kiaroa Eco-Luxury Resort

Bahia, Brazil

Blinding white unspoilt sandy beaches, coco palm trees, mangrove forests and crystal-clear blue shimmering water – the Kiaroa Lodge has everything that you dream of in a tropical paradise. The 28 room hotel set in South Bahia on the Marau peninsula can also only be reached by boat, which makes the dream of the tropics ideal. The water of the eco-lodge is heated by solar power, the wood for building the bungalows comes from certified reforestation programmes, and the furniture finished by local craftsmen.

Blendend weiße unverbaute Sandstrände, Kokospalmen, Mangrovenwälder und kristallklares blau schimmerndes Wasser - die Kiaroa Lodge hat alles, was man sich von einem tropischen Paradies erträumt. Zudem ist das im Süden Bahias auf der Halbinsel Marau gelegene 28-Zimmer-Hotel nur mit dem Boot erreichbar, was den Tropentraum perfekt macht. Das Wasser der Eco Lodge wird mit Solarstrom erhitzt, das Holz für den Bau der Bungalows kommt aus zertifizierten Aufforstungsprogrammen, die Möbel wurden von einheimischen Handwerkern gefertigt.

Des plages de sable blanc étincelant, vierge de toute construction, des cocotiers, des forêts de mangroves et une eau bleue étincelante et cristalline. Le Lodge Kiaroa possède tous les ingrédients d'un paradis tropical. De plus, cet hôtel de 28 chambres installé au sud de Bahias, sur la presqu'île de Marau, ne peut être rejoint qu'en bateau. Le rêve tropical est ainsi complété ! L'eau de ce lodge écologique est chauffée par l'énergie solaire, le bois utilisé dans la construction des bungalows provient de programmes de reforestation certifiés et les meubles ont été construits par des artisans locaux.

El Kiaroka Lodge tiene todo lo que se puede soñar de un paraíso tropical: playas vírgenes de arena blanca, cocoteros, manglares y aguas aguas celestes cristalinas. Además, el hotel de 28 habitaciones situado al sur de Bahía, en la Península de Marau, sólo es accesible en barco, lo que hace perfecto el sueño tropical. El agua del alojamiento ecológico se calienta con energía solar. La madera para la construcción de los bungalows proviene de programas certificados de reforestación y los artesanos locales han realizado los muebles.

Spiagge deserte di sabbia bianca accecante, palme di noci di cocco, boschi di mangrovie e acqua cristallina dai riflessi azzurri – il Kiaroa Lodge possiede tutto ciò che si può sognare per un paradiso tropicale. Per questo l'hotel di 28 camere che si trova sulla penisola di Marau, a sud di Bahia, può essere raggiunto soltanto via mare, con un battello, come si addice ad un perfetto sogno ai tropici. L'acqua nell'eco-lodge viene riscaldata con energia solare, il legno per le costruzioni dei bungalows proviene da zone protette da programmi di rimboschimento certificati, i mobili sono stati costruiti da artigiani indigeni.

A tropical atmosphere that stressed city people dream about.

Ein tropisches Ambiente, das gestresste Stadtmenschen zum Träumen bringt.

Une ambiance tropicale qui fera rêver l'homme urbain stressé.

Un ambiente tropical que invita a soñar al estresado hombre de ciudad.

Un paesaggio tropicale che fa sognare i turisti stressati dalla vita in città.

Tauana

Bahia, Brazil

An endlessly long unspoilt sandy beach on the bay of Corumbau, shielded from the rain forest that almost reaches the coast. On these magnificent beauty spots the Portuguese architect Ana Catarina built the nine 130 square-meter light-flooded cabanas at this exclusive eco-resort. The interior cultivates a brazilian minimalistic-chic. The water is solar-heated, waste is recycled or composted, the precious mangoes grow on the trees, and herbs come from the gardens.

Ein endlos langer unverbauter Sandstrand an der Bucht von Corumbau, abgeschirmt vom Regenwald, der fast bis zur Küste vordringt. An diesen traumhaften Flecken Erde baute die portugiesische Architektin Ana Catarina die neun 130 Quadratmeter großen, lichtdurchfluteten Cabanas ihres exklusiven Eco Resorts. Das Interieur kultiviert einen minimalistischen brasilianischen Chic. Das Wasser ist solargeheizt, Abfall wird recycelt oder kompostiert, die köstlichen Mangos wachsen auf den eigenen Bäumen, Kräuter kommen aus dem Garten.

Une immense plage de sable fin, vierge de toute construction, entoure la baie de Corumbau. Elle est protégée par la forêt tropicale qui atteint presque le bord de mer. Sur ce petit coin de paradis terrestre, l'architecte portugaise Ana Catarina a construit neuf bungalows, baignés de lumière, de 130 m² chacun, créant ainsi ce complexe hôtelier écologique exclusif. L'aménagement intérieur est placé sous le signe du minimalisme chic brésilien. L'eau chaude est obtenue par l'énergie solaire, les déchets sont recyclés ou compostés, de merveilleuses mangues poussent aux arbres et les épices proviennent du jardin.

Se trata de una interminable playa de arena virgen en la Cala de Corumbau, protegida por la selva que llega casi hasta la costa. La arquitecta portuguesa Ana Catarina construyó en esta pedazo del paraíso las transparentes 9 cabañas de 130 metros cuadrados que conforman su esclusivo resort ecológico. El interior cultiva un elegante minimalismo brasileño. El agua se calienta con energía solar, la basura se transforma en compost, los deleiciosos mangos crecen en los propios árboles y las hierbas provienen del jardín.

Una spiaggia deserta e sconfinata sulla baia di Corumbau, riparata dalla foresta tropicale che si spinge quasi fino alla costa. In questo punto fantastico della terra l'architetto portoghese Ana Catarina ha costruito questi nove cabanas, di 130 metri quadri ciascuno, che con i loro teli filtrano la luce del sole e che formano il suo esclusivo eco-resort. Gli interni si ispirano ad un elegante stile minimalista brasiliano. L'acqua viene riscaldata da energia solare, i rifiuti vengono riciclati o compostati, gli alberi di mango forniscono frutti squisiti, le verdure sono coltivate nell'orto.

The minimalist-chic of the interior design sets a striking counterpoint to the rampant lush beauty of the rainforest.

Der reduzierte Chic des Interior Design setzt einen markanten Kontrapunkt zur wuchernden Üppigkeit des Regenwalds.

Le chic minimaliste de la décoration intérieure est un singulier contraste avec la luxuriance de la forêt tropicale.

La reducida elegancia del diseño interior crea un profundo contraste con la exuberancia de la selva.

L'eleganza minimalista del disegno degli interni crea un contrasto deciso con la rigogliosa foresta tropicale.

Explora Rapa Nui

Easter Island, Chile

Easter Island is one of the most magical places in the world. It is located 3.800 kilometres away from the Chilean mainland in the expanse of the Pacific, guarded by stone giants. Building a hotel in this sensitive environment poses a particular challenge. The efforts that Explora took to make the Posada de Mike Rapu as environmentally friendly as possible, by using local volcanic stone, sustainable heat insulation, and a light concept with huge windows that minimize artificial light, were rewarded in 2009 with the U.S. environmental commendation LEED.

Die Osterinsel ist einer der magischsten Orte auf dieser Welt. 3 800 Kilometer vom chilenischen Festland entfernt in den Weiten des Pazifiks, bewacht von steinernen Giganten. In dieses sensible Umfeld ein Hotel zu bauen, bedeutet eine besondere Herausforderung. Die Anstrengungen, die Explora unternahm, die Posada de Mike Rapu möglichst umweltschonend zu erstellen, mit heimischem Vulkanstein, nachhaltiger Wärmedämmung, einem Lichtkonzept mit riesigen Fenstern, die künstliches Licht minimieren, wurden 2009 mit dem US-amerikanischen Umweltprädikat LEED belohnt.

L'île de Pâques est l'un des recoins magiques de ce monde. Distante de 3800km du Chili continental, en plein océan Pacifique, elle est surveillée par ses géants de pierre. Construire un hôtel dans cet environnement sensible est un véritable défi. Les efforts déployés par Explora pour construire la Posada de Mike Rapu avec un impact environnemental minimum, en utilisant la pierre volcanique locale, une isolation thermique durable, un concept d'éclairage basé sur d'immenses baies vitrées qui réduisent le recours à l'éclairage artificiel, ont été récompensés en 2009 par la concession du prix américain de l'environnement LEED.

La Isla de Pascua es uno de los lugares más mágicos del Mundo. A 3.800 kilómetros del Chile continental en el Pacífico y custodiada por gigantes de piedra. Construir un hotel en este sensible entorno constituyó un reto especial. Los esfurzos realizados por Explora para construir la Posada de Mike Rapu cuidando al máximo el medio ambiente, con piedra volcánica local, un aislamiento térmico duradero y un concepto de iluminación basado en enormes ventanas que reduce al máximo el uso de electricidad, se vieron premiados en 2009 con la mención de calidad estadounidense LEED.

L'Isola dell'Est è uno dei luoghi più magici al mondo. A 3 800 chilometri dalla terraferma del Cile, al largo dell'Oceano pacifico, sorvegliata da giganti di pietra. Costruire un hotel in questo ambiente delicato è stata una sfida particolarmente difficile. Explora si è molto impegnata per rendere minimo l'impatto della Posada de Mike Rapu sull'ambiente, adoperando pietra vulcanica del luogo, un sistema per conservare a lungo il calore, un progetto per l'illuminazione che grazie a enormi finestre riducesse al minimo la luce artificiale; tutti questi sforzi le sono valsi il titolo LEED degli Stati Uniti per l'attenzione verso l'ambiente.

The cult sites of the indigenous people on the Southwest tip of the island shaped the curved architecture of the hotel building.

Die Kultstätten der Einheimischen am Südwestzipfel der Insel gaben die Formen vor für die geschwungene Architektur des Hotelbaus.

La culture autochtone de la pointe sud-ouest de l'île a donné naissance aux formes arquées de l'architecture de l'édifice.

Las ciudades sagradas de los nativos en la punta sudoeste de la isla inspiraron las formas que impulsaron la arquitectura del hotel.

Gli insediamenti religiosi degli indigeni, all'estremità sud-occidentale dell'isola, hanno suggerito le forme per l'architettura ricurva dell'edificio dell'hotel.

Three Camel Lodge

Gobi, Mongolia

The Three Camel Lodge in the Gobi desert intends to resurrect the Nomad culture. Guests live in yurt tents traditionally made from felt and wooden sticks, as was customary in Mongolia for centuries until the former Communist rule. Furniture has been built and painted by local craftsmen using traditional models. At night you can hear "Hoomi" throat singing with the endless vastness of the desert sky over you.

Die Kultur der Nomaden wiederbeleben, will die Three Camel Lodge in der Wüste Gobi. Gäste wohnen in traditionell aus Filz und Holzstangen gebauten Jurte-Zelten, wie es in der Mongolei über Jahrhunderte üblich war, bevor die ehemals kommunistischen Herrscher das Nomadenleben verboten. Die Möbel wurden von einheimischen Handwerkern nach überlieferten Vorbildern gebaut und bemalt. Nächtens kann man den tief aus der Kehle kommenden Hoomi-Gesängen lauschen, während sich die unendliche Weite des Wüstenhimmels über einem spannt.

Réveiller la culture nomade est l'objectif du Lodge Three Camel, dans le désert de Gobi. Les vacanciers habitent dans les traditionnelles yourtes, des tentes construites avec des barres en bois et du feutre, selon la manière traditionnelle en vigueur depuis des siècles en Mongolie. Du moins jusqu'à ce que les autorités communistes interdisent la vie nomade ! Les meubles ont été fabriqués et peints par des artisans autochtones, selon des modèles qui leur ont été fournis. La nuit venue, vous écouterez les chants gutturaux des Hoomi, alors que l'immensité de la voûte céleste du désert vous recouvre.

El Three Camel Lodge del Desierto de Gobi pretende recuperar la cultura de los nómadas. Los visitantes se alojan en las tradicionales yurtas hechas con un entramado de madera y fieltro, como ha sido habitual durante siglos en Mongolia antes de que los comunistas prohibieran la vida nómada. Artesanos locales han costruido y pintado los muebles siguiendo modelos tradicionales. Se pueden escuchar las canciones Hoomi que surgen de la profundidad de la garganta, mientras se despliega la eterna inmensidad del cielo del desierto.

Al Three Camel Lodge nel deserto del Gobi si vuole ridare vita alla cultura dei nomadi. Gli ospiti alloggiano nelle tende jurte costruite come da tradizione con pali di legno e feltro di lana; così per secoli avevano vissuto i Mongoli prima che i capi comunisti vietassero la vita nomade. I mobili sono stati costruiti e dipinti da artigiani del luogo secondo modelli tramandati nei secoli. Di notte si possono ascoltare i canti hoomi con i loro toni profondi, mentre sul lodge si dispiega l'infinito cielo stellato del deserto.

Living as a nomad - this experience is possible in the Mongolian Lodge.

Leben wie ein Nomade — diese Erfahrung lässt sich in der mongolischen Lodge machen.

Vivre comme les nomades; cette expérience est rendue possible dans les Lodge mongoles.

En este alojamiento mongol es posible experimentar la vida nómada.

Vivere come un nomade — nel lodge mongolo si può fare.

176   Three Camel Lodge *Gobi, Mongolia*

Crosswaters Ecolodge & Spa

Guangzhou, China

As a prototype for sustainable tourism, China's first eco lodge was designed in Nankunshuan nature reserve, two and a half hours north east of Hong Kong. It is built entirely from fast-growing bamboo. Even on arrival the path over the bamboo bridge gets you in the right frame of mind to leave the hectic pace of everyday life far behind you. The 46 guest houses have been positioned according to Feng Shui principles directly on the riverside. In the Tai Chi studio amidst the bamboo grove inner balance can be restored.

Als Prototyp für nachhaltigen Tourismus wurde Chinas erste Ecolodge im Nankunshuan Naturreservat, zweieinhalb Stunden nordöstlich von Hongkong, konzipiert. Sie ist gänzlich aus dem schnell wachsenden Bambus gebaut. Schon bei der Ankunft stimmt der Weg über die Bambusbrücke darauf ein, die Hektik des Alltags weit hinter sich zu lassen. Die 49 Gästehäuser wurden nach modernen Feng Shui-Prinzipien direkt am Flussufer positioniert. Im Tai Chi Studio mitten im Bambushain lässt sich die innere Balance wieder herstellen.

Le lodge écologique, situé dans la réserve naturelle de Nankunshuan, a été conçu comme un prototype du tourisme durable en Chine; il est à deux heures et demie au nord-est d'Hong Kong. Il a été entièrement construit dans le bambou local à croissance rapide. Dès votre arrivée, le pont en bambou menant au lodge vous invitera à laisser le stress quotidien derrière vous. Les 49 bungalows sont situés directement au bord du fleuve et construits selon les principes du feng shui moderne. Dans le studio Tai Chi, installé au milieu d'un bocage de bambou, vous parviendrez à rétablir votre équilibre intérieur.

Concebido como prototipo para turismo sostenible, se construyó en China el primer alojamiento ecológico en la Reserva Natural de Nankunshuan, a dos horas y medis al norte de Hong kong. Está construido sólo de bambú, que crece rápidamente. Ya a la llegada, el camino por el puente de bambú invita a dejar atrás el ajetreo de la vida cotidiana. Las 49 casa están situadas justo en la orilla del río, siguiendo los principios del feng shui moderno. En medio del bosque de bambú, el estudio de tai chi le permite recuperar el equilibrio interior.

Il primo eco-lodge della Cina, nella riserva naturale di Nankunshuan, a due ore e mezzo di viaggio a nord-est di Hongkong, è stato ideato come prototipo per un turismo che duri nel tempo. E' interamente costruito in bambù, che qui cresce velocemente. Già all'arrivo, attraversando il ponte di bambù, si ha la sensazione di lasciare completamente dietro di se' il ritmo frenetico della vita di tutti i giorni. Le 49 abitazioni per gli ospiti sono state costruite direttamente sulla riva del fiume, secondo i moderni principi del feng shui. Nel Tai Chi Studio, in mezzo al boschetto di bambù, si può ricreare il proprio equilibrio interiore.

The position directly on the river was chosen carefully—guests should be able to feel a part of nature.

Die Lage direkt am Fluss wurde mit Bedacht gewählt: Gäste sollen sich als Teil der Natur erleben können.

Cette implantation directement au bord du fleuve n'est pas due au hasard: les visiteurs doivent pouvoir faire corps avec la nature.

Su situación en el río se ha escogido cuidadosamente: el visitante debe poder integrarse en la naturaleza.

La posizione vicino al fiume è stata accuratamente studiata: gli ospiti devono potersi sentire parte integrante della natura.

Six Senses Hideaway Yao Noi

Amphur Koh Yao, Phang-Nga, Thailand

The view from the sweeping terraces to the Phang Nga bay with its bizarre limestone rocks rising vertically out of the glassy water surface is breathtaking. The journey by boat takes nearly an hour from the airport of Phuket to the island of Yao Noi. The 56 wood-constructed guest villas of the Six Senses Hideaway cultivate the idea of intelligent luxury. The building materials come from the region or are recycled while fabrics are unbleached and naturally dyed.

Der Blick von den weitläufigen Terrassen auf die Phang Nga Bucht mit ihren bizarren Kalkfelsen, die sich senkrecht aus der spiegelglatten Wasserfläche erheben, ist atemberaubend. Eine knappe Stunde dauert die Fahrt mit dem Boot vom Flughafen Phuket zur Insel Yao Noi. Die 56 aus Holz konstruierten Gästevillen des Six Senses Hideaway kultivieren die Idee des intelligenten Luxus. Auf Überflüssiges wird verzichtet, die Baumaterialien kommen aus der Region oder sind recycelt, Stoffe ungebleicht und pflanzengefärbt.

Le panorama de cette étendue de terrasses au-dessus de la baie de Phang Nga et de leurs curieux rochers de calcaire, surgissant à la verticale d'une mer lisse comme un miroir, est époustouflant. Le trajet en bateau reliant l'aéroport Phuket à l'île Yao Noi dure une petite heure. Les 56 bungalows construits en bois du Six Senses Hideaway, cultive l'idée du luxe intelligent. L'on a volontairement renoncé au superflu, les matériaux de construction proviennent de la propre région ou ont été recyclés, les étoffes n'ont pas été traitées par blanchiment et les teintures de leurs coloris sont d'origine végétale.

Es impresionante la vista desde las terrazas a dos niveles sobre la Cala de Phang-Nga, con sus imponentes rocas de cal que se alzan perpendiculares a la cristalina superficie del agua. El trayecto en barco desde el aeropuerto de Phuket zur a la Isla Yao Noi dura escasamente una hora. Las 56 villas construidas en madera del Six Senses Hideaway, cultivan la idea del lujo inteligente. Se ha renunciado a todo lo superfluo. Los materiales de construcción son locales o reciclados. Los tejidos no han sido tratados con lejía y los tintes son vegetales.

Dalle ampie terrazze si spazia sulla baia di Phang Nga con le sue bizzarre rocce calcaree che spuntano dalla superficie dell'acqua liscia come uno specchio, la veduta è così straordinaria da togliere il respiro. Poco meno di un'ora dura il viaggio in battello che dall'aeroporto di Phuket raggiunge l'isola di Yao Noi. Nelle 56 ville per gli ospiti del Six Senses Hideaway, tutte costruite in legno, si realizza l'idea di arredare con lusso ma in modo intelligente. Tutto ciò che è superfluo è stato eliminato, i materiali edili provengono dalla regione o sono riciclati, i tessuti non vengono candeggiati e sono tinti con coloranti vegetali.

The raw-timber spacious guest villas give a certain „back to nature" feeling.

Die roh gezimmerten großzügig dimensionierten Gästevillen vermitteln ein gewisses „Zurück-zur-Natur"-Gefühl.

Les bungalows destinés aux clients sont de généreuses dimensions. Les ébauches de charpenterie génèrent une impression de « retour aux sources ».

Las despejadas y amplias villas proporcionan un sentimiento de retorno a la naturaleza.

Le ville per gli ospiti, costruite in modo grezzo ma di dimensioni straordinarie, trasmettono una certa sensazione di „ritorno alla natura".

Anantara Si Kao Resort & Spa

Si Kao, Thailand

A magical water wonderland by landscape designer Bill Bensley runs through the whole resort. Wellness programmes with a focus on Ayurveda and yoga emphasize the holistic approach. Programmes on energy and water saving are managed in a comprehensive "Green Project". The herbs for the deliciously light restaurant cuisine come from the hotel's own gardens.

Das ganze Resort durchzieht eine verwunschene Wasserlandschaft des Landschaftsdesigners Bill Bensley. Wellnessprogramme mit dem Schwerpunkt auf Ayurveda und Yoga unterstreichen den ganzheitlichen Ansatz. In einem umfangreichen „Green Project" sind Programme zum Energie- und Wassersparen geregelt. Die Kräuter für die köstlich leichte Restaurantküche kommen aus dem hoteleigenen Garten.

L'ensemble du complexe hôtelier est traversé par un magnifique paysage aquatique dessiné par l'architecte paysager Bill Bensley. Des programmes de bien-être mettant l'accent sur la méthode Âyurveda et le yoga, marque l'accent de l'ensemble. Les programmes d'économie d'énergie et d'eau sont englobés dans un vaste « Green Project ». Les épices utilisées dans la merveilleuse cuisine, savoureuse et légère du restaurant, proviennent du propre jardin du complexe hôtelier.

Todo el resort pasa por un paisaje acuático del diseñador Bill Bensley. Los programas de Spa resaltan el principio global, con Ayurveda y Yoga como punto fuerte. Los programas de ahorro de agua y energía se incluyen en un "Proyecto verde". Las hierbas utilizadas en la exquisita y ligera cocina del restaurante crecen en su jardín.

L'intero resort si ispira all'incantevole paesaggio d'acqua elaborato dal designer paesaggista Bill Bensley. Programmi per il benessere incentrati sulla filosofia ayurveda e yoga mettono in evidenza l'idea basilare del progetto. In un grande "green project" come questo sono stati ovviamente elaborati anche programmi per il risparmio dell'energia e dell'acqua. Le verdure per la squisita cucina leggera del ristorante sono coltivate nell'orto dell'hotel.

The terraces of the 138 rooms and suites overlook the calm Andaman Sea and its limestone rocks.

Von den Terrassen der 138 Zimmer und Suiten schaut man über die sanfte Andamansee und ihre Kalkfelsen.

Depuis les terrasses des 138 chambres et suites, les clients ont une magnifique vue sur le lac Andaman et sur les rochers de calcaire.

Desde las terrazas de las 138 habitaciones y suites se puede contemplar el mar de Andamán y sus rocas de cal.

Dalle terrazze delle 138 camere e suite si può spaziare sulle dolci acque del mare di Andaman e sulle sue rocce calcaree.

Alila Villas Soori

Bali, Indonesia

Southwest Bali was formerly the home of the royal family of Tahaban. In December 2009 the Alila Group opened the first luxury hotel on the southwest coast, not far from the palace that tells of the former wealth of the royal house. In constructing the 48 pool villas designed in a cool modern design the strict eco-standards of Green Global were followed. Choice of building materials, energy efficiency, waste minimization, protection of species and involvement in social programmes - all of this is taken into consideration by the Alila philosophy.

Der Südwesten Balis war früher Sitz der königlichen Familie von Tahaban. Nicht weit vom Palast, der vom einstigen Reichtum des Könighauses erzählt, eröffnete die Alila Gruppe Dezember 2009 das erste Luxushotel an der Südwestküste. Beim Bau der 48, in einem coolen modernen Design gestalteten Poolvillen wurden die strengen Ökostandards von Green Globe eingehalten. Wahl der Baumaterialien, Energieeffizienz, Abfallminimierung, Artenschutz und Engagement in sozialen Programmen – all das schließt die Alila-Philosophie ein.

Le sud-ouest de Bali était jadis le siège de la famille royale de Tahaban. Non loin du palais, témoin de l'ancienne splendeur de la maison royale, le groupe Alila a inauguré en décembre 2009 le premier hôtel de luxe de la côte sud-ouest. Les plus strictes normes écologiques de Green Globe ont été respectées lors de la construction des 48 bungalows avec piscine, aménagés dans un design moderne et simple. La philosophie du groupe Alila inclut le choix des matériaux de construction, l'efficacité énergétique, la minimisation des déchets, la conservation des espèces et l'engagement dans des programmes de nature sociale.

En el Sudoeste de Bali estaba antiguamente la corte de la familia real de Tahaban. No muy lejos del palacio, que deja entrever la pasada riqueza de la familia real, el grupo Alila abrió en diciembre de 2009 el primer hotel de lujo de la costa sudoeste. En la construcción de las 48 villas con piscina decoradas con un moderno diseño, se han contemplado los estrictos estándares de Green Globe. La filosofía de Alila abarca la elección de los materiales de construcción, la eficacia energética, la reducción de los desechos, la protección de la biodiversidad y el compromiso con los programas sociales.

La parte sud-occidentale di Bali un tempo era sede della famiglia reale di Tahaban. Sulla costa sud-occidentale, non lontano dal palazzo che testimonia la ricchezza di un tempo della casa reale, nel mese di dicembre 2009 il gruppo Alila ha aperto questo primo hotel di lusso. Nella costruzione delle 48 ville con piscina, progettate secondo un design moderno sono stati rispettati i severi standard ecologici del Green Globe. Selezione dei materiali edili, efficienza energetica, riduzione dei rifiuti, protezione delle specie ed impegno in programmi sociali – questo prevede la filosofia dell'Alila.

The newly opened boutique hotel has the effect of a cool new modern statement against the rampant exotic kitsch.

Wie ein kühles modernes Statement gegen den grassierenden Exotik-Kitsch wirkt das neu eröffnete Boutiquehotel.

Ce nouvelle boutique-hôtel, récemment inauguré, semble être une déclaration fraîche et moderne contre le traditionnel kitsch exotique.

La boutique del hotel, de nueva apertura, es una afirmación moderna contra el estendido kitsch exótico.

Questo hotel-boutique, aperto recentemente, sembra voler essere un fresco proclama moderno contro il kitsch esotico dilagante.

Wolgan Valley Resort & Spa

Wolgan Valley, Australia

The Wolgan Valley Resort & Spa at the foot of the Blue Mountains scores high with the endless expanse and solitude of the Australian outback. The sheep farms as built by the first Australian settlers provided the model for the resort's architecture. The resort opened at the end of 2009, which consists of low buildings that are firmly nested in the landscape. Local building materials that save on natural resources were used, demonstrating the highest standard of environmental technology. In the hotel's own nature reserve reforestation is being carried out to restore the natural balance of flora and fauna.

Mit der unendlichen Weite und Einsamkeit des australischen Hinterlands punktet das Wolgan Valley Resort & Spa am Fuße der Blue Mountains. Vorbild für die Architektur des Ende 2009 eröffneten Resorts lieferten die Schaffarmen, wie sie die ersten australischen Siedler bauten. Niedrige Gebäude, die sich förmlich in die Landschaft hinein ducken. Verwendet wurden heimische, die natürlichen Ressourcen schonende Baumaterialien, die Umwelttechnologie weist den höchsten Standard auf. Im hoteleigenen Naturreservat wird mit Aufforstungen daran gearbeitet, die natürliche Balance der Flora und Fauna wiederherzustellen.

Les immenses étendues et la solitude de l'arrière-pays australien permettent au Wolgan Valley Resort & Spa, installé au pied des Blue Mountains, de marquer des points. Le modèle pour l'architecture de ce complexe hôtelier, ouvert à la fin de l'année 2009, a été les fermes des élevages de moutons, construits par les premiers colons australiens. Les paysages bas se fondent réellement dans le paysage. L'utilisation de matériaux de construction, respectueux des ressources naturelles et la technologie écologique utilisée, est la preuve de la haute qualité de l'ensemble. La réserve naturelle propre du complexe s'emploie à rétablir l'équilibre naturel entre la flore et la faune en effectuant des opérations de reforestation.

Con la gran inmensidad y soledad del Continente australiano, deslumbra el Wolgan Valley Resort & Spa a los pies de Las Montañas Azules. Ejemplo de la arquitectura de los resort abiertos a finales de 2009 son los crearon los Schaffarmen, tal y como construían los primeros colonos de Australia. Los edificios bajos se adaptan a las formas del paisaje. Se utilizan materiales de construcción locales, con recursos naturales y la tecnología medioambiental cuenta con los más altos niveles de calidad En la reserva natural del propio hotel se trabaja con reforestación para recuperar el equilibrio natural de la flora y la fauna.

Gli spazi sconfinati e l'isolamento dell'entroterra australiano sono i valori aggiunti del Wolgan Valley Resort & Spa ai piedi delle Blue Mountains. Le antiche costruzioni dei primi coloni australiani hanno fatto da modello per l'architettura di questo resort, aperto alla fine del 2009. Sono bassi edifici dalle forme ricurve che si piegano verso il terreno. Per il resort sono stati adoperati materiali del luogo che risparmiano le risorse naturali ed una tecnologia ambientale che raggiunge i più alti standards. Nella riserva naturale che appartiene all'hotel si sta procedendo a lavori di rimboschimento per ricreare l'equilibrio naturale della flora e della fauna.

The comfortable suites invite you to relax after extensive mountain walks in the Greater Blue Mountains or a trek in the Wolgan Valley.

Nach ausgedehnten Bergtouren in die Greater Blue Mountains oder einem Ausritt ins Wolgan Valley laden die komfortablen Suiten zur Entspannung ein.

Après de longues excursions dans les Greater Blue Mountains ou une promenade à cheval dans la Wolgan Valley, les suites confortables invitent au délassement.

Tras amplios paseos por la montaña en las Grandes Montañas Azules o un paseo en el Wolgan Valley, las cómodas suites invitan al relax.

Le suites dotate di ogni confort invitano gli ospiti al relax dopo lunghe escursioni nelle Blue Mountains o dopo una passeggiata nella Wolgan Valley.

Hapuku Lodge and Tree Houses

Kaikoura, New Zealand

How does the world look from a bird's eye view? This can be experienced in one of the five tree houses at the Hapuku Lodge on the South Island of New Zealand. Architect and owner Tony Wilson built the wooden guest houses on 10 meter high stilts in the tree tops of the Manuka trees - in one of the most spectacular landscapes in New Zealand. The snow-covered tops of the Kaikura Mountains light up in the background, and not far away is the enticing Mangamaunu surfing bay.

Wie schaut die Welt aus der Vogelperspektive aus? Das lässt sich in einem der fünf Baumhäuser der Hapuku Lodge auf der Südinsel Neuseelands erleben. Architekt und Besitzer Tony Wilson hat die aus Holz konstruierten Gästehäuser auf zehn Meter hohe Stelzen in die Wipfel der Manuku-Bäume gebaut – in eine der spektakulärsten Landschaften Neuseelands: Im Hintergrund leuchten die schneebedeckten Gipfel des Kaikura Gebirges, nicht weit davon lockt die Surfer-Bucht Mangamaunu.

À quoi ressemble le monde à vue d'oiseau ? C'est ce que vous pourrez découvrir dans l'une des cinq fermes du Lodge Hapuku installé au sud de la Nouvelle-Zélande. Tony Wilson, l'architecte et propriétaire, a construit les bungalows en bois, destinés aux clients, sur des pilotis de 10m de hauteur, dans les cimes des arbres manuku, dans l'un des paysages les plus spectaculaires de la Nouvelle-Zélande : en arrière-plan, les cimes couvertes de neige du massif Kaikura et, non loin de là, la baie de Mangamaunu, paradis des surfeurs.

¿Cómo se ve la Tierra desde la perspectiva de un pájaro? Esto se puede experimentar en una de las cinco casas en los árboles del Hapuku Lodge en la Isla Sur de Nueva Zelanda. El arquitecto y propietario Tony Wilson ha construido las casas a 10 metros de altura en la copa de los árboles Manuka, uno de los paisajes más espectaculares de Nueva Zelanda, Pues al fondo relucen las cumbres nevadas de los Montes Kaikura, y no muy lejos se encuentra la cala de Mangamaunu para hacer surf.

Come potrebbe essere il mondo visto dalla prospettiva degli uccelli? Nelle cinque case sull'albero dell'Hapuku Lodge sull'Isola del Sud della Nuova Zelanda si può provare anche questa avventura. Il proprietario, l'architetto Tony Wilson ha costruito queste case in legno su palafitte alte 10 metri, nelle chiome degli alberi chiamati Manuku – in uno dei paesaggi più spettacolari della Nuova Zelanda: sullo sfondo splendono le cime innevate del monte Kaikura, non lontano da qui la baia di Mangamaunu richiama gli amanti del surf.

For those who are afraid of heights the five ground-floor suites offer a welcome alternative.

Für alle, die nicht schwindelfrei sind, bieten die fünf ebenerdigen Suiten eine willkommene Alternative.

Pour tous ceux qui souffrent de vertige, cinq suites au niveau du sol proposent une heureuse alternative!

Aquellos que tengan vértigo, tienen en las cinco suites a nivel de suelo una buena alternativa.

Le cinque suites a terra offrono un'accogliente alternativa per tutti gli ospiti che soffrono di vertigini.

Cousteau Fiji Islands Resort

Fiji

A Garden of Eden and one of the last paradises in the world. Nowhere else does the crystal-clear water shimmer in soft pastel turquoise colors; nowhere else is the sand more powdery and white than on the Fijian islands. The multi award-winning resort situated on Vanua Levu island is making great efforts to preserve this precious heritage—from the protection of abutting coral reefs and the hotbeds of turtles to the careful treatment of resources even in the smallest areas.

Ein Garten Eden und eines der letzten Paradiese auf dieser Welt. Nirgendwo schimmert das glasklare Wasser in pastelligeren Türkistönen, nirgendwo ist der Sand puderiger und weißer als auf den Fiji-Inseln. Um dieses kostbare Erbe zu bewahren, unternimmt das auf der Insel Vanua Levu gelegene, mit renommierten Umwelt-Preisen ausgezeichnete Resort vielfältige Anstrengungen: vom Schutz des vorgelagerten Korallenriffs und der Brutstätten der Schildkröten bis zum Ressourcen schonenden Umgang auch in den kleinsten Bereichen.

Un jardin d'Éden et l'un des derniers paradis de ce monde. Nulle part ailleurs vous ne verrez une eau si cristalline, teintée de couleur pastel turquoise, et nulle part ailleurs le sable sera plus fin et plus blanc que dans les îles Fidji. Pour préserver ce précieux héritage, ce complexe hôtelier situé sur l'île Vanua Levu, récompensé par de nombreux prix écologique, a entrepris de gros efforts : depuis la protection de la barrière de corail au large de la plage et lieu de couvaison des tortues, jusqu'à la gestion consciencieuse des ressources naturelles, même jusque dans les plus petits détails.

Nos encontramos ante un Jardín del Edén y uno de los últimos paraísos del Mundo. En ningún otro sitio el agua transparente brilla tanto en tonos turquesa, ni la arena es tan fina y blanca como en las islas Fiji. Para conservar esta valiosa herencia el resort, situado en la Isla Vanua Levu y condecorado con numerosos premios medioambientales, toma numerosas medidas: desde la protección de los arrecifes de coral y los caparazones de las tortugas hasta un cuidadosos tratamiento de los recursos, incluso los de menor importancia.

Un giardino dell'Eden ed uno degli ultimi paradisi del pianeta. In nessun altro luogo l'acqua trasparente riluce di riflessi così turchesi, in nessun altro luogo la sabbia è così fine e bianca. Per conservare questa preziosa eredità delle isole Fiji il resort Cousteau, che si trova sull'isola di Vanua Levu e che è stato insignito con rinomati premi per la tutela dell'ambiente, ha messo in atto numerose iniziative: dalla protezione della barriera corallina antistante all'isola e dei luoghi di cova delle tartarughe fino a progetti risparmino le risorse naturali anche nei più piccoli settori della gestione.

The 25 bures (as the thatched-roof huts on the Fiji islands are called) are furnished in typical rattan style of the South Seas.

Die 25 Buren, wie die traditionell mit Reet gedeckten Holzhütten auf den Fijis heißen, sind südseetypisch mit Rattanmöbeln eingerichtet.

Les 25 cabanes traditionnelles couvertes de chaume, dénommées « buren » aux Fidji et typiques des mers du Sud, sont aménagées avec des meubles en rotin.

Los 25 buren, como se denominan en las islas Fiji las tradicionales cabañas de madera cubiertas con juncos, están decoradas con muebles de rattán, como es típico en Los Mares del Sur.

Le 25 bure, così vengono chiamate le capanne di legno dal tradizionale tetto di canne sulle isole Fiji, sono arredate con mobili di rattan secondo lo stile tipico dei mari del sud.

Index

Sweden

Åre

Copperhill Mountain Lodge

Åre Björnen, 83013 Åre, Sweden
Phone: +46 / 647 / 143 00, Fax: +46 / 647 / 143 98
www.copperhill.se
Price category: $$
Rooms: 112 hotel rooms and suites, most rooms with terrace
or balcony and view of the mountain landscape
Facilities: Restaurants, bars, Samí inspired spa, six conference
rooms
Services: Childminding, free shuttle bus within Åre, WiFi,
ski rental
Ecological Features: Use of regionally and sustainably
produced raw ingredients from 200 km radius, built almost
entirely with local materials, geothermal heating system without
CO_2 emission, the lightning is automatically turned off when
leaving the room, use of low-energy lamps, waste is sorted and
sent for recycling.

United Kingdom

Cornwall

The Scarlet

Trenance, Mawgan Porth, Newquay, Cornwall TR8,
United Kingdom
Phone: +44 / 1637 / 86 18 00, Fax: +44 / 1637 / 86 18 01
www.scarlethotel.co.uk
Price category: $$
Rooms: 37 rooms, two have been designed for disabled access
Facilities: Ayurvedic spa, restaurant
Services: Wedding service
Ecological Features: Heating by biomass, pools and flushing
toilets sourced from rainwater, sustainability director, reducing
waste involving also suppliers and sub-contractors, reusing and
recycling all items possible, indoor swimming pool heated by
solar panels (or biomass boiler), biomass boiler run on sustainable
wood chips heating the hotel, energy saving ventilation system
rather than use of air conditioning units, high levels of insulation
reducing heat loss, electricity supplied by ecological provider is
100% from renewable sources, car sharing by staff, "buy local,
buy responsible" policy, supporting actively local social and
environmental projects, beach cleans at Mawgan Porth beach,
working with local schools and colleges, providing advice and
information for other businesses.

Austria

Längenfeld

Naturhotel Waldklause

Unterlängenfeld 190, 6444 Längenfeld, Austria
Phone: +43 / 52 53 / 54 55, Fax: +43 / 52 53 / 545 54
www.waldklause.at
Price category: $$
Rooms: 50 rooms
Facilities: Therm "Aquadome" , restaurant, Finnish sauna, gym,
sun terrace, tennis courts, relaxation room, parking garage
Services: Internet, steam bath, herb bath, free mountain bikes
and hiking sticks, guided walking-tours
Ecological Features: Built of natural local materials, biological
procedural methods only, heating with wood chips, using local
herbs for spa products.

Leogang

Priesteregg

Sonnberg 22, 5771 Leogang, Austria
Phone: +43 / 65 83 / 82 55 20, Fax: +43 / 65 83 / 825 54
www.priesteregg.at
Price category: $$
Rooms: Chalets with two bedrooms, living room, kitchen,
chimney, terrace, Hot Pot, wellness bathtub and shower
Facilities: Modern kitchen, restaurant nearby
Services: Internet, TV, bicycle and walking-tours, archery,
horse riding, tandem flex-wing flights, snowshoeing, village fairs,
massage and beauty treatments
Ecological Features: No cars allowed in the village, interior
and exterior seating out of reused wood from old local
farmhouses, high insulation, use of local material for construction,
use of untreated wood, heating with eco-friendly wood chips,
use of natural products for spa treatments, manufacturing of
many F&B products inhouse.

France

Gargas

La Coquillade

Relais & Châteaux La Coquillade, Hameau Perrotet
84400 Gargas, France
Phone: +33 / 490 / 74 71 71, Fax: +33 / 490 / 74 71 72
www.coquillade.fr
Price category: $$$
Rooms: 6 houses with 7 rooms, 7 junior suites and 14 suites,
private terraces or gardens
Facilities: 2 restaurants: Le Gourmet with terraces, Le Bistrot
with garden, snackbar at the swimming pool, salon-bar,
outdoor lounge, boutique, bike rental, swimming pool, tennis
and pétanque courts, old-timer renting, meeting rooms,
wine cellar
Services: TV, DVD, WiFi, iPod stations, hairdryer, safe
Ecological Features: Geothermal heating and cooling system
avoids CO_2 emission, 27 drillings of 100 m depth, solar panels
generate heat for the pool, waste water recycling, own
electrical production by gaz-turbines with heat-recuperation.

Greece

Chania, Crete

Milia Mountain Retreat

73012 Vlatos, Kissamos, Chania, Crete, Greece
Phone: +30 / 28 210 / 467 74, Fax: +30 / 28 220 / 515 69
www.milia.gr
Price category: $
Rooms: 16 rooms with fireplaces or woodstoves and balcony,
small terrace or garden
Facilities: Restaurant, meeting room, parking, WiFi
Services: Lessons in traditional Cretan cooking, wine-tasting
sessions, seminars on the interesting local flora, all the above
over agreement with extra charge and not all year round,
several walking paths for trekking, mountain bikes (for
experienced bikers only), free participation in farm activities
Ecological Features: Houses restored from the ruins of the
medieval neighbourhood of Milia, products from own organic
countryside, solar energy, reforestation of the area, support the
local culture and economy, total remote site, eco matresses beds.

Italy

Contrada Verdura Sciacca, Sicily

Verdura Golf & Spa Resort

Contrada Verdura Sciacca, Sicily 92019, Italy
Phone: +39 / 0925 / 99 81 80, Fax: +39 / 0925 / 99 81 83
www.verduraresort.com
Price category: $$$
Rooms: 203 rooms with view across the Mediterranean Sea from private terrace
Facilities: Restaurants, bars, golf courses, spa, pool, meeting rooms, ballroom, amphitheatre, tennis courts
Services: 24 h business center, video conferencing, latest audiovisual equipment, WiFi in meeting rooms, secretarial and translation services, worldwide courier services, on-site travel agency, yoga class
Ecological Features: Designed incorporating the latest building technology to protect the surrounding environment, solar panels, double-glazed bedroom windows to maximise energy conservation, use of low energy lightbulbs, coast protection programmes prevent erosions, solar panels provide electricity, electric cars only are allowed on the resort, strict recycling policy.

Gargnano

Lefay Gargnano

Via Angelo Feltrinelli, 118, 25084 Gargnano, Italy
Phone: +39 / 0365 / 24 18 00, Fax: +39 / 0365 / 24 18 99
www.lefayresorts.com
Price category: $$$
Rooms: 90 rooms
Facilities: Terrace or balcony with view on Lake Garda, restaurant, bar, bistro
Services: Internet, TV
Ecological Features: Power is generated from renewable energy sources, DIN certified bio architecture (ISO 14001 and ISO 9001), natural regional materials in all rooms, bed-linen from untreated cotton, chemical-free wall colors, no WiFi in order to avoid electro-smog, mobile shading system, wood chips bio heating system, heat insulating glazing, use of rainwater, recycling of pool water for irrigation, photovoltaics on the roof is also used for shading, recycling of waste, software for saving of energy and water.

Alpe di Siusi, South Tyrol

Seiser Alm Urthaler

39040 Alpe di Siusi, South Tyrol, Italy
Phone: +39 / 0471 / 72 79 19, Fax: +39 / 0471 / 72 78 20
www.seiseralm.com
Price category: $$
Rooms: 51 rooms and 3 suites
Facilities: Wine cellar, restaurant, bar, gym, „Antermoia – beauty, sports & bath", parking garage, meeting room, spacious panoramic indoor pool with outdoor pool, Finnish sauna, steam baths, cosmetic treatments, massages, Alps regeneration garden
Services: Guided walking-tours, free golf trial courses, mountainbike rental, ski rental, Internet
Ecological Features: Construction of the hotel shows excellent thermal insulation, wood provides optimal air moisture and a cosy temperature of the rooms and the inside surfaces, built of used timber structures without any chemical substances and without adhesive, rooms are free of electro-magnetic fields and radiation.

San Cassiano, Alta Badia, South Tyrol

Lagació Mountain Residence

Micurà De Rü, 48, 39030 San Cassiano, Alta Badia
South Tyrol, Italy
Phone: +39 / 0471 / 84 95 03, Fax: +39 / 0471 / 84 93 86
www.lagacio.com
Price category: $$$
Rooms: 24 premium apartments ranging from 42 m² to 88 m² with panorama windows. Three storeys furnished in larch, swiss pine or spruce
Facilities: LA PALSA wellness area, Finnish sauna, steam bath, low-temperature sauna, fitness room, cosmetic treatments, massages and baths
Services: Shopping crate, organic box, valuable tips on activities (ski, mountainbike, golf), events and culinary experiences, booking of mountaineering or skiing tours, adventurous family outings or helicopter flight over the Dolomite peaks
Ecological Features: High level of insulation, certified climate house A-standard, low energy consumption, energy-efficient, environment-friendly, healthy, technical and electrical systems ensure that energy requirements for heating are less than 30 kWh/m² per year, the water from the Residence's own spring is revitalised according to the Grander method (Grander's water revitalisation technique returns the water molecules to their original, highly ordered state, thus improving water quality).

Spain

Tudela

Hotel Aire de Bardenas

Ctra. de Ejea, Km. 1,5, 31500 Tudela, Spain
Phone: +34 / 948 / 11 66 66, Fax: +34 / 948 / 11 63 48
www.airedebardenas.com
Price category: $$
Rooms: 18 rooms and 4 deluxe suits, rooms with private exterior patio with fruit tree and exterior bathtub
Facilities: Meeting rooms with IT support, restaurant with garden
Services: Internet, TV, laptops for rent, 24 h room service, booking of segway outings, paintball, cultural visit in Tudela, horse riding, mountain biking, canoeing
Ecological Features: Located in the Bardenas Reales Nature Reserve, barriers against the strong winds built with recycled wood containers, built of recycled materials, solar panels heat the water, no cement, camouflaged without disturbing the landscape, ecological garden for the restaurant fertilized by organic waste, water saving irrigation, protection of migrant birds.

Santa Eulalia, Ibiza

Quilibria Aguas de Ibiza

C/Salvador Camacho n°9, Ibiza, Spain
Phone: +34 / 971 / 31 99 91, Fax: +34 / 971 / 31 98 60
www.aguasdeibiza.com
Price category: $$$
Rooms: 86 rooms and 26 suites
Facilities: Spa, bar, restaurant, lounge, terrace, pool, garden, spa suite, event halls
Services: WiFi, 24 h room service
Ecological Features: Use of renewable energies and efficiency, use of 35 percent less energy than comparable hotels in the luxury segment, Domotics control system allows highly efficient light and temperature settings.

Egypt

Siwa

Adrère Amellal

Siwa, Egypt
Phone: +202 / 2736 / 78 79, Fax: +202 / 2735 / 54 89
www.adrereamellal.net
Price category: $$$
Rooms: 40 rooms
Facilities: Restaurant
Services: Lunch is served by the pool, dinner somewhere different every day, desert excursions and day trips to the historical sites of Siwa, massages, horse riding
Ecological Features: Built with indigenous material using traditional techniques with minimal impact on the environment and maintaining indoor temperatures, ceilings made of palm beams, doors and windows made of olive wood from annual tree trimmings, wastewater settled in self-contained sedimentation tanks, the supernatant flows into a sealed wetland watering indigenous papyrus plants that complete the biodegradation, most of the food organically grown and local, no electricity, indoor heating with coal-filled braziers, natural ventilation systems, organic agriculture, producing very limited noise.

Jordan

Wadi Araba

Feynan Ecolodge

Dana Biosphere Reserve, Wadi Araba, Jordan
Phone: +962 / 6464 / 55 80, Fax: +962 / 6464 / 55 85
www.feynan.com
Price category: $
Rooms: 26 rooms, each with ensuite washroom
Facilities: Terraces, rooftop terrace (ideal for stargazing), library lounge with fireplace, restaurant with indoor and outdoor dining, meeting/conference facilities, gift shop
Services: Excursions, hiking, canyoning, mountain biking
Ecological Features: Located in the Dana Biosphere Reserve, the largest nature reserve in Jordan where endangered species such as the Syrian wolf, Nubian ibex, and the finely marked desert cats are protected from extinction, providing socioeconomic opportunities for local Bedouin communities, generating revenue for the conservation of Jordan's wild places, considered a pioneer for eco-tourism projects in Jordan, exclusively solar powered and illuminated by candles at night, composting food waste and recycling other waste.

United Arab Emirates

Liwa Desert, Abu Dhabi

Qasr Al Sarab Desert Resort by Anantara

Liwa Desert, Abu Dhabi, United Arab Emirates
Phone: +971 / 28 86 20 88, Fax: +971 / 28 86 20 86
www.qasralsarab.anantara.com
Price category: $$$
Rooms: 206 rooms, suites and villas
Facilities: 3 restaurants, bar, Anantara Spa, health club, 3 tennis courts, kids club, business facilities, library, pool
Services: Nature & wildlife excursions, guided desert walks, archery, camel trekking, falconry, entertainment system, WiFi
Ecological Features: Built with natural materials, carefully inserted in the landscape considering the wandering of the dunes, furniture designed with local wood, Experience Center for guests introducing the sensitive ecosphere of the desert, damped lightening by night, support of the local population by donating revenues from the hotel's boutique craft sales to the Red Cross.

Musandam Peninsula, Oman

Six Senses Hideaway Zighy Bay

Zighy Bay, Musandam Peninsula, Sultanate of Oman
Phone: +968 / 267/ 358 88, Fax: +968 / 267/ 358 87
www.sixsenses.com/Six-Senses-Hideaway-Zighy-Bay
Price category: $$$$
Rooms: 79 pool villas plus The Private Reserve and 2 retreats
Facilities: Large central pool, Six Senses Spa with nine treatment rooms and juice bar, 2 Arabian Hamams, Zighy Souk Oman market, library with WiFi and wide selection of movies, CDs, DVDs, books and magazines, gym, Six Senses gallery, 1.6 km private sandy beach, 2 bars, 3 restaurants, "Meeting Lounge" for up to 8 people
Services: Limousine transfers to and from the airport, poolside service offering gourmet meals, beverages and home made ice creams, non-motorized water-sports, multi lingual hosts, on site nurse, gym instructor, wide range of activities within the Resort and excursions to places in Musandam and the surrounding regions, beach service, butler service by villa team
Ecological Features: The detailed Environment Management Program monitors the respectful treatment of the environment, stones from the Hadschar Mountains were used for building the villas and the hotel.

Tanzania

Mahale Mountains National Park

Greystoke Mahale

Mahale Mountains National Park, Tanzania
Phone: +49 / 6081 / 68 84 89 (Exclusive Travel Choice)
www.greystoke-mahale.com, www.nomad-tanzania.com
Price category: $$$$
Rooms: 6 open-fronted banda with dressing rooms behind and upstairs chill-out decks
Facilities: Bar, en-suite bathroom with hot and cold water, flush toilets and powerful showers
Services: Hikes into the forest in search of the chimpanzees, other primates, bushbuck, bushpig, and amazing birds and butterflies, fishing, kayaking out into the lake or along the shoreline, beach dinners under the stars, sundowners on the dhow
Ecological Features: Nature reserve prohibiting hunting and protecting and researching the lives of chimpanzees and of other monkeys, protection of the rainforest along the shore of Lake Tanganjika in the Mahale-region, furniture and interiors made from old Arabian sailing vessels and from dugout canoes, textiles originate from local weaving mills, craftsmanship is locally produced, access not by car or plane but only by ship.

Botswana

The Okavango Delta

Xaranna Okavango Delta Camp

The Okavango Delta, Botswana
Phone: +002 / 67 / 683 03 42
www.andbeyondafrica.com/luxury_safari/botswana/okavango_delta/and_beyond_xaranna
Price category: $$$
Rooms: Nine en-suite tents with sala, private plunge pool, indoor bathtub and al fresco shower, maximum 18 people
Facilities: Xaranna Okavango Delta Camp has its own delta island within 25.000 hectare, open sided dining room, Safari Shop, reading spots
Services: Safaris in the open 4x4 safari vehicles, on boats and mekoros (traditional dugout canoe), guided walking tours
Ecological Features: Release of endangered species such as black rhinos avoiding extinction, protection of the dying tropical forest, the lodge is built on stilts reducing the impact of linear foundations, inverter system to provide power to the rooms but saving up to 30% on generator time.

Seychelles

North Island

North Island

North Island, Indian Ocean, Seychelles
Phone: +248 / 29 31 00, Fax: +248 / 29 31 50
www.north-island.com
Price Category: $$$$
Rooms: 11 villas with lounge and plunge pool
Facilities: Restaurant, beach bar, spa with outdoor area, PADI dive center, gym, 4 beaches including a private honeymoon beach
Services: Individually created cuisine, each villa is equipped with an electro-buggy and 2 bicycles.
Ecological Features: Establishment of a Rehabilitation Plan (this is imperative as the Island is covered by 55% alien vegetation and this is one of the major constraints to fauna reintroduction) with development of an indigenous vegetation nursery, flora and fauna reintroduction process, Environmental Impact Assessment (EIA) for the proposed development, the EIA fed into the lodge design (i.e. no bright lights on the beach because of turtle hatchings etc.), waste separation and recycling, vegetable and herb garden, no fishing offered - fishing is only for consumption, conservation projects of a team of biologists and ecologists that is permanently based on the island.

Madagascar

Tsarabanjina Island

Constance Lodge Tsarabanjina

Tsarabanjina Island, Madagascar
Phone: +261 / 3205 / 152 29
www.tsarabanjina.com
Price category: $$
Rooms: 25 bungalows with private terrace, main bedroom equipped with fans, bathroom with shower and separate WC, private terrace with deck chairs and coffee table
Facilities: Bar, tennis courts, table tennis, shop with a wide range of Malagasy art and handmade craft items, line of clothing of Tsarabanjina
Services: Healthy diet made up mainly of sea food, snorkeling, kayaking, water-skiing, sailing, volleyball, bocci games, fishing, excursions to discover the Mitsio Archipelago, massage and reflexologie, transfer from Nosy Be, safe, telephone via satellite, telephone network for mobile phones, Internet access, doctor on call
Ecological Features: No air-conditioning in the bungalows, preservation of the species requiring protection, respect of the protection of the environment (guests are advised not to take shells, not catch sharks during fishing excursions), no lobsters during the season break, no burning or burying of rubbish, divided rubbish bins (separation of paper, plastic, glass and others), most of the food bought locally.

Mozambique

Benguerra Island

Benguerra Lodge

Benguerra Island, Mozambique
Phone: +27 / 11 / 452 06 41, Fax: +27 / 11 / 452 14 96
www.benguerralodge.co.za
Price category: $$$
Rooms: 30 guests in 2 Cabanas, 10 Casitas: private pool and deck, fans / Villa Chibuene: personal chef / Villas at Benguerra: satellite television, audio system, book collection, rooftop terrace, fully equipped kitchen
Facilities: Gift shop, lounge and bar, dining room, indoor and outdoor seating areas, pool, spa
Services: Scuba diving, snorkeling, comprehensive Medical Rescue Insurance (flight to Johannesburg in under 2 hours), fishing, dhow cruises, castaway picnics, landrover trips, bird watching, island walks, village visits, sea kayaking, catamaran cruises, horse riding, personal butler-service in the Casitas
Ecological Features: Located on the Bazaruto Archipelago - one of a few national marine parks in the world, guests are accompanied during snorkelling and diving in order to protect the coral reef, for fishing there is a strict policy of "catch & release", cooperation with the WWF in protection of turtles and the very rare Dugongs, financing of social projects such as primary schools or hospitals with a part of the overnight rate.

Republic of Namibia

Kaokoland

Okahirongo Elephant Lodge

Kaokoland, Republic of Namibia
Phone: +264 / 65 / 68 50 18, Fax: +264 / 65 / 68 50 19
www.okahirongolodge.com
Price category: $$$
Rooms: 18 guests
Facilities: Restaurant, swimming pool, several lounges, open fireplace, driving range
Services: Game and Nature drives, sunrise and sunset drives, hiking trails in and around the Hoarusib Valley, elephant drives, bird watching, Desert Lion Project, visits of the local Himba Village
Ecological Features: Research project for desert lions, protection of the walkways for the desert elephants through the Hoarusib rivier, training program for local people in jobs on all levels of the lodge, removal of all waste from the lodge by lorry, selling of handcrafts produced by the local Himbas.

Wolwedans, NamibRand Nature Reserve

Boulders Safari Camp

Wolwedans, NamibRand Nature Reserve, Republic of Namibia
Phone: +264 / 61 / 23 06 16, Fax: +264 / 61 / 22 01 02
www.wolwedans.com
Price category: $$$
Rooms: 4 tents on wooden platforms
Facilities: Dining and lounge tent, breakfast deck, open fireplace
Services: Guided tours on foot and by car
Ecological Features: Located on former farmland that has been renaturalised and fences have torn down, farm animals have been relocated in order to return the wildlife to their natural living, tents have been built according to ecological criteria without encroaching on nature, water out of bor holes in the desert, solar panels for warm water, no private cars allowed within the Private Nature Reserve.

South Africa

Hermanus

Grootbos Forest Lodge

Hermanus, South Africa
Phone: +27 / 28 / 384 80 00, Fax: +27 / 28 / 384 80 40
www.grootbos.com
Price category: $$
Rooms: 16 luxury suites with lounge, ensuite bathroom, veranda
Facilities: Forest Lodge with restaurant, champagne bar, wine cellar for private dinners, pool, modern conference center, suits with bathroom, separate lounge with fireplaces, private deck
Services: Whale watching, shark cage diving, horse riding, nature drives and walks, birding, beach activities
Ecological Features: Set in a nature reserve, built in an ecological way, foundation protecting the valuable and exceptionally rich variety of Feynbos flora (as the unique flora at the Cape is called), guests are involved in projects of social responsibility like a gardener school or sport facilities in the township of Gansbaai.

USA

California

El Capitan Canyon

11560 Calle Real, Santa Barbara CA 93117, USA
Phone: +1 / 805 / 685 38 87, Fax: +1 / 805 / 968 67 72
www.elcapitancanyon.com
Price category: $$
Rooms: 108 cedar cabins, 26 safari tents, 5 canyon yurts
Facilities: Heated pool
Services: Massage treatments, beach cruiser bikes available
Ecological Features: Solar panels provide lighting and heat the pool, rescue programme for trees uprooted by storms in order to avoid using them as firewood, replanting native habitat along the creek, recycling bins, nontoxic cleaning products.

Wyoming

Amangani

1535 North East Butte Road, Jackson, WY 83001, USA
Phone: +1 / 307 / 734 73 33, Fax: +1 / 307 / 734 73 32
www.amanresorts.com/amangani_homes.aspx
Price category: $$$$
Rooms: 40 suites, Amangani Homes with 4 bedrooms and spacious living and dining areas
Facilities: Spa, health center, whirlpool, heated outdoor pool
Services: Electrical phone, cable television/high-speed internet, private water system with a 600,000 gallon tank and piped-in natural gas, private cars and drivers available, hiking, biking, horse riding, cross-country skiing
Ecological Features: Built from local building materials, recycling of all paper, glass and plastic, avoid using plastic bottles, water filter system allows to reuse the glass bottles provided in the guest rooms, some of the roofs cropped with grass for isolation, monthly financial support for the "Jackson Hole Conservation Alliance" that buys private land in order to conserve it wild and avoid construction.

Caribbean

St. Lucia

Anse Chastanet

St. Lucia, Caribbean
Phone: +1 / 758 / 459 70 00
www.ansechastanet.com
Price category: $$$
Rooms: 37 hillside rooms
Facilities: Piti Piton Bar, the Treehouse Restaurant, Trou au Diable beach restaurant, 2 beaches
Services: Spa, yoga, fitness, scuba diving, snorkelling, excursions, jungle biking, bird watching
Ecological Features: Constructed with maximum use of local materials and exclusively with local labor, built around the trees, glassless windows replace air condition, independent water supply from the community in order not to burden the community, resurrection of water reservoir from 18th century for water rain and river water used for irrigation, regular monitoring of water consumption, organic produce from resort farm, using non-toxic cleaning products, reduced use of paper, protection of marine area, only natural lighting by day, employees rewarded for taking fuel-efficient transport to work, recycling wherever possible, biodegradable care products, providing education and sustainable information programs for employees, integrating guests in the environmental protection efforts and social and cultural activities, employing local people.

Dominica

Jungle Bay Resort & Spa

Point Mulatre, Commonwealth of Dominica, West Indies
Phone: +1 / 767 / 446 17 89, Fax: +1 / 767 / 446 10 90
www.junglebaydominica.com
Price category: $$
Rooms: Cottages with spacious patio with views of the jungle (some with premium ocean view)
Facilities: 2 indoor yoga studios, bar, recreation lounge with movie library and big-screen DVD player, dart board, pool table, table tennis and plenty of games, sun deck, spa, restaurant
Services: Telephone and small refrigerator in the cottages, safety deposit boxes in main office
Ecological Features: Constructed utilizing sustainably harvested wood & local materials, cottages on wooden posts to reduce and minimize disturbance on the soils, architecture avoids energy consumption by eliminating the need for lighting or air conditioning, restaurant serves 95% locally grown organic food, local guides trained in responsible travel techniques take guests on guided educational tours, re-usable water bottles for guests decrease use of disposable bottles, annual beach cleaning, sea turtle conservation program.

Bahamas

Tiamo

South Andros Island, Bahamas
Phone: +1 / 242 / 369 23 30, Fax: +1 / 242 / 376 44 08
www.tiamoresorts.com
Price category: $$$$
Rooms: 11 cottages - Pool Cottage with Jacuzzi and private decking, Cool Cottage with bar and walk-in wardrobe, Island Breeze Cottage with walk-in showers
Facilities: Lodge "The Great Room", library, beach deck, pool, private beach, restaurant with terrace, spa, gym
Services: Diving, snorkelling, sailing, nature tours, wedding service, fishing
Ecological Features: Constructed with lowest possible impact on nature, clearing the construction site using machetes, not machinery, all energy from solar panels, roofs are thatched to retain coolness and insulate, some cottages with air condition run by bio fuel, white roofs reflect the sun rays, water for the private Jacuzzis heated by the sun.

Mexico

Tulum

Azulik

Tulum, Mexico
Phone: +54 / 11 / 59 18 64 00, Fax: +54 / 11 / 59 18 64 99
www.azulik.com
Price category: $$$
Rooms: 15 private beachfront villas with view of the Caribbean Sea and large private deck
Facilities: Maya Hanging beds, wooden outside bathtub, spa, Temazcal (indigenous sweat lodge), Healing massage
Services: Room service, electronic safe in the villa
Ecological Features: No electricity, no telephone, no TV, huts timbered from local wood, low-flow shower and toilets heads in all bathrooms, conservation of biological diversity and cultural diversity is practiced.

Costa Rica

Turrialba

Pacuare Lodge

Turrialba, Costa Rica
Phone: +506 / 2225 / 39 39, Fax: +506 / 2253 / 69 34
www.pacuarelodge.com
Price category: $$$
Rooms: 19 guest bungalows
Facilities: Main lodge with sprawling terrace
Services: Wedding service, canopy tour, canyoneering (combination of hiking, climbing and rappelling), massage treatments, horse riding, Cabécar Indians Tour, "Plant a tree program", car rentals, white water rafting, honeymoon packages
Ecological Features: Built with minimal impact of the surrounding, no trees cutted, the lodge bought 300 hectares (740 acres) that was destined for deforestation, all staff from local communities, financial support and environmental education program for 8 schools in the communities nearby, cultural rescue program for Cabécar Indians, thatch roofs made by local Cabécar Indians, no electricity in lodge and bungalows, use of organic and locally-grown products, reforesting with native tree species to offset carbon emissions, sponsoring a jaguar monitoring program, reintroducing monkeys wiped out in the area by indigenous hunters, "reduce, reuse and recycle" program, composting organic waste, use of biodegradable detergent, solar-heated water, biodigester at the lodge to process organic waste and sewage into energy-producing methane gas to heat water and provide electricity, use of a small electricity-generating water-driven turbine using a local water source to avoid the use of fossil fuel.

Peru

Colca Canyon

Las Casitas del Colca

Parque Curiña s/n Yanque, Arequipa, Peru
Phone: +51 / 54 / 959 67 24 80, Fax: + 51 / 1 / 242 33 65
www.lascasitasdelcolca.com
Price category: $$$
Rooms: Casitas with spacious lounge, large bathroom, floor heating, private terrace and heated plunge pool
Facilities: Spa, restaurant, animal farm, bar, vegetable garden
Services: Bird Watching, horse riding, walking tours, trekking, cycling, cookery lessons
Ecological Features: Built with local materials, in the hotel's own gardens fruit and vegetable are grown, organic waste is composted and recycled, waste water sent to a treatment plant to ensure that any water released into the environment is 100% clean, laundry water passes through a separate treatment to remove traces of detergent.

Peru

Lake Titicaca

Titilaka

Lake Titicaca, Peru
Phone: +51 / 1 / 700 51 05, Fax: +51 / 1 / 700 51 29
www.andean-experience.com
Price category: $$$$
Rooms: 18 fully serviced lake-view suites with heated floors, spa bathrooms, oversized tubs, massage showers, 24 h room service, concierge, WiFi, safe, writing desk, cordless phones, iPod dock
Facilities: Massage room, lounge, dining room, bar with wraparound terraces overlooking the lake, fully equipped communication center or media room with TV
Services: Activities including mysticism, adventure, nature, archaeology, cultural or artistic events, community related visits, family-oriented activities and living cultures with private vehicle and driver, bilingual full or part-time guide, Experience Concierge, kayaking, hiking, sailing, nanny and medical service
Ecological Features: Electricity comes from renewable energy sources, a sophisticated concept reduces waste.

Brazil

Bahia

Kiaroa Eco-Luxury Resort

Loteamento da Costa, área SD6, Dist. de Barra Grande, Município de Maraú, CEP 45.520-000 - Bahia, Brazil
Phone: +55 / 73 / 32 58 62 13, Fax: +55 / 73 / 32 58 62 13
www.kiaroa.com.br
Price category: $$$
Rooms: 14 rooms and 14 bungalows
Facilities: Spa, restaurant, natural pools, bar, beach bar, pool, tennis court, beach volleyball, bikes, game room and lounge for reading and relaxation, business center with WiFi, boutique and convenience store, private airstrip, helipad
Services: Turn down service, VIP lounge at Salvador's International Airport, boat and land excursions
Ecological Features: Water heated by solar power, a part of the hotel uses solar energy, the wood for construction of the buildings comes from certified reforestation programmes, the furniture has been finished by local craftsmen.

Bahia

Tauana

Corumbau, Bahia, Brazil
Phone: +55 / 73 / 36 68 51 72, Fax: +55 / 73 / 36 68 51 72
www.tauana.com
Price category: $$$$
Rooms: 9 cabanas
Facilities: Restaurant, Helipod, WiFi
Ecological Features: Solar-heated water, waste is recycled or composted, cultivating of own fruits and herbs in the gardens, reforestation project, sewage treatment system.

Chile

Easter Island

Explora Rapa Nui

Casas Rapa Nui, Sector Te Miro Oone s/n
Casilla 31, Correo Isla de Pascua, Easter Island
Phone: +56 / 562 / 395 27 00, Fax: +56 / 32 / 10 01 39
www.explora.com/explora-rapa-nui
Price category: $$$$
Rooms: 30 rooms with ocean view and hydromassage bath
Facilities: Pool, heated Jacuzzi, bar, restaurant
Services: Massage treatments - relaxation and therapeutic, lodge shop (special clothing, gear for exploring , books, handicrafts and jewelry)
Ecological Features: Built with local volcanic stone, sustainable heat insulation, the light concept with huge windows minimises artificial light, rewarded with the US environmental commendation LEED.

Mongolia

Gobi

Three Camel Lodge

Gobi, Mongolia
Phone: +976 / 11 / 31 33 96, Fax: +976 / 11 / 32 03 11
www.threecamellodge.com
Price category: $
Rooms: 30 standard and 20 deluxe gers (traditional felt tents of Mongolia's nomadic herders) with private bathroom with a toilet and sink, equipped with king size beds
Facilities: Bulagtai Restaurant, Thirsty Camel Bar, Conference Hall and equipments, spa, small library, laundry
Services: Music and dance performances, wildlife viewing trips, camel treks through sand dunes and forests, hiking, horse treks, biking, hunting for Dinosaur Fossils, cooking lessons, visiting local nomads
Ecological Features: Tents traditionally made from felt and wooden sticks, furniture built and painted by local craftsmen using traditional models, organic local food served in the restaurant, light bulbs fueled by solar and wind energy, non-drinking water re-used, trash transported and recycled, active cooperation and constant interaction with local government, NGOs and schools to preserve the nature in the Gobi.

China

Guangzhou

Crosswaters Ecolodge & Spa

Mt. Nankun Ecotourism District Longmen,
Guangdong 516876 China
Phone: + 86 / 752 / 769 36 66, Fax: +86 / 752 / 769 31 56
www.crosswaters.net.cn
Price category: $
Rooms: 50 guest rooms
Facilities: Chinese style restaurant, western style restaurant, forest spa, meeting rooms, outdoor swimming pool
Services: Treatments based on environmental friendly principles
Ecological Features: China's first eco-lodge, design and construction comply with Green Globe 21 standards, located in the Nankunshuan nature reserve, built entirely from fast-growing bamboo, positioned according to Feng Shui principles, locally sourced food.

Thailand

Amphur Koh Yao, Phang-Nga

Six Senses Hideaway Yao Noi

56 Moo 5, Tambol Koh Yao Noi, Amphur Koh Yao,
Phang-Nga 82160, Thailand
Phone: +66 / 76 / 41 85 00, Fax: +66 / 76 / 41 85 18
www.sixsenses.com/Six-Senses-Hideaway-Yao-Noi
Price category: $$$$
Rooms: 56 guest villas with pool, sundeck, DVD player, satellite TV and working desk
Facilities: Bar and restaurants, wine cabinet
Services: Butler Service, air conditioning, outdoor daybeds (can be converted for sleeping at night time), electronic safe, IDD telephone with data line access, in-house clinic, Six Senses Gallery and jewelry shop, library with internet access, music and movie library, airport transportation service, flowers, gifts, romantic dinner at a private location, bubble bath, express laundry services
Ecological Features: Building materials came from the region or are recycled, fabrics are unbleached and naturally dyed, rainwater is collected and processed by water treatment plant for use in toilets and irrigation, a big part of furniture and lamps are made of recycled material (for example of driftwood).

Si Kao

Anantara Si Kao Resort & Spa

Sikao, Thailand 198-199 Moo 5 Had Pak Meng - Changlang Road, Changlang beach, Maifad Si Kao, Trang 92150 Thailand
Phone: +66 / (0)7520 / 58 88, Fax: +66 / (0)7520 / 58 99
http://sikao.anantara.com
Price category: $$
Rooms: 138 rooms and suites with satellite TV, DVD player, oversized bathtubs and private balconies overlooking the ocean or the Bill Bensley-designed tropical landscape, suites with private plunge pools, LCD TV, iPod docking station, Anantara Private Villa with private 28 square meter pool, private bar, 24 h service
Facilities: Anantara Spa, pool bar, 2 indoor and outdoor restaurants, lounge café, private beach club
Services: Wedding service, dine by design (dinner on sandbank, on the beach, in the forest, garden or herb garden with personal chef), sailing, waterskiing, kayaking, windsurfing, canoeing and other water sports, diving, snorkelling
Ecological Features: Energy and water saving, compost production of food remnants to fertilize plants and vegetables, re-use of waste water for irrigation after filtering, recycling, herb garden around the resort, beach cleaning by staff and management, green diversion for guests (while kayaking the guests can help to keep the mangroves green and without waste), local community support (mangrove plantation project).

Indonesia

Bali

Alila Villas Soori

Banjar Dukuh, Desa Kelating, Kerambitan, Tabanan,
Bali 82161, Indonesia
Phone: +62 / 361 / 894 63 88, Fax: +62 / 361 / 894 63 77
www.alilahotels.com/soori
Price category: $$$$
Rooms: 48 pool villas with private pool
Facilities: Spa, restaurant, pool, beach cabanas
Services: Leisure concierges, Alila Gallery, 24 h clinic
Ecological Features: Constructed following the eco standards of Green Global, choice of building materials, energy efficiency, waste minimisation, protection of species and involvement in social programmes.

Australia

North Queensland

Daintree Eco Lodge

20 Daintree Road, Daintree QLD 4873, North Queensland,
Australia
Phone: +61 / 7 / 40 98 61 00, Fax: +61 / 7 / 40 98 62 00
www.daintree-ecolodge.com.au
Price category: $$$
Rooms: 15 guest villas with fully micro-screened balcony, TV, CD player, direct dial telephone, air-conditioning and ceiling fan, spa Villas with jacuzzi on micro-screened balcony
Facilities: Spa, restaurant, art gallery, undercover pool with sun deck
Services: Wedding service, Aboriginal cultural activities, transfer services, WiFi (in public areas and some villas), free in-house movies
Ecological Features: Guest villas built from local wood, involvement of the Aboriginal people in the project.

Wolgan Valley

Wolgan Valley Resort & Spa Australia

2600 Wolgan Road, Wolgan Valley, Lithgow,
NSW 2790, Australia
Phone: +61 / 2 / 63 50 18 00, Fax: +61 / 2 / 63 50 18 01
www.emirateshotelsresorts.com/wolgan-valley
Price category: $$$$
Rooms: 40 suites with iPod docking station, high-speed Internet access, private, temperature controlled pool (4x7 m), pool deck, courtyard garden (veranda 168 square metres), kitchen, dining room, double-sided fireplace, lounge area, walk-in dressing room, central air-conditioning, LCD TV, DVD player and sound system, international TV channels
Facilities: Restaurant, spa
Services: Horse Riding, nature walks, mountain biking, wildlife safaris, historical tours, 24 h room service, mountain bikes, binoculars, in-room safe, same-day laundry/dry-cleaning service
Ecological Features: Constucted using local building materials that save on natural resources, highest standard of environmental technology, own nature reserve reforestation, 4,000 acres of land dedicated as a wildlife reserve securing indigenous and endangered species, comprehensive conservancy programme for animals and plants.

New Zealand

Kaikoura

Hapuku Lodge and Tree Houses

State Highway 1 at Station Road, RD 1, Kaikoura, New Zealand
Phone: +64 / 3 / 319 65 59, Fax: +64 / 3 / 319 65 57
www.hapukulodge.com
Price category: $$$
Rooms: 5 Lodge Suites with fireplaces, balconies; 5 Tree houses
Facilities: Meeting room facility, lounge, restaurant, bar, terrace, outdoor solar heated swimming pool and sauna
Services: Marine safari, whale watching, sea kayaking, deep-sea fishing, Maori cultural tours, helicopter flights, winery tours, horse riding, biking, hiking, surfing, skiing, fishing, Night Sky Tour, Golf, private dining
Ecological Features: Located in Kaikoura, a community internationally recognized for its environmental efforts, surrounded by an expansive deer farm and 1,000 tree olive grove, handcrafted furniture, the lodge plants one native plant for every guest night spent there, water heated by solar energy, recycling and composting waste, replacing incandescent light bulbs with compact fluorescents, using sustainable materials whenever possible, sourcing food from local organic farmers, "Discover Kaikoura's Maori Culture" and "Bush Restoration" programs for guests.

Fiji Islands

Fiji

Cousteau Fiji Islands Resort

Vanua Levu, Fiji
Phone: + 415 / 788 / 57 94 (from USA),
+61 / 3 / 98 15 03 79 (from Australia),
Fax: +415 / 788 / 01 50 (from USA),
+61 / 3 / 98 15 22 71 (from Australia)
www.fijiresort.com
Price category: $$$$
Rooms: 25 bures
Facilities: Spa, restaurant, tennis courts, pool
Services: Wedding service, village excursions, rain forest hikes to waterfalls, mangrove adventures, reef flat walks, basket weaving, Fijian story telling, Niumaia's Medicinal Plant Walk, volleyball, snorkeling, scuba diving, kayaking, fishing, glass bottom boat, Fijian music, kava ceremonies, traditional medicines, visits of neighbour village, Fiji slide presentations, visit at farmer's market
Ecological Features: Multi eco-award-winning resort, protection of abutting coral reefs and the hotbeds of turtles, conservation and community support, first-ever winner of "Australasia's Leading Green Hotel", organic gardens, built with renewable materials, guest education, hosting medical clinics for Fijians, Fiji's first and only water reclamation plant using naturally occurring and recycled materials as filter mediums, Giant Clam restoration program, iniciated establishing the world-acclaimed Namena Reef as a protected area.

Photo Credits

Produced by fusion publishing gmbh, berlin
www.fusion-publishing.com

Edited by Patricia Massó, fusion publishing

Editorial coordination by Manuela Roth, fusion publishing;
Bettina Schlösser, teNeues Verlag

Texts by Bärbel Holzberg

Translations by Bochert Translation

Layout by Manuela Roth

Imaging & prepress by fusion publishing gmbh

Production by Sandra Jansen, teNeues Verlag

Published by teNeues Publishing Group

teNeues Verlag GmbH & Co. KG
Am Selder 37, 47906 Kempen, Germany
Tel.: 0049-(0)2152-916-0, Fax: 0049-(0)2152-916-111
E–mail: books@teneues.de

Press department: arehn@teneues.de
Tel.: 0049-(0)2152-916-202

teNeues Publishing Company
16 West 22nd Street, New York, NY 10010, USA
Tel.: 001-212-627-9090, Fax: 001-212-627-9511

teNeues Publishing UK Ltd.
21 Marlowe Court, Lymer Avenue, London, SE19 1LP, Great Britain
Tel.: 0044-208-670-7522, Fax: 0044-208-670-7523

teNeues France S.A.R.L.
39, rue de Billets, 18250 Henrichemont, France
Tel.: 0033-2-48269348, Fax: 0033-1-70723482

www.teneues.com

© 2010 teNeues Verlag GmbH + Co. KG, Kempen

ISBN: 978-3-8327-9370-8

Printed in Czech Republic